DO YOU WANT TO BE A HEALER/PSYCHIC?

Bric-a-brac I have collected to help you develop your abilities

Elizabeth R.

Copyright © 2020 Elizabeth R Gelhard

All rights reserved

The characters and events portrayed in this book are fictitious. Any similarity to real persons, living or dead, is coincidental and not intended by the author.

No part of this book may be reproduced, or stored in a retrieval system, or transmitted in any form or by any means, electronic, mechanical, photocopying, recording, or otherwise, without express written permission of the publisher.

ISBN-13: 9798617794405
ISBN-10: 1477123456

Cover design by: Art Painter
Library of Congress Control Number: 2018675309
Printed in the United States of America

CONTENTS

Title Page
Copyright
Chapter 1 Spirit Prods   1
Chapter 2 Meeting Angels, Guides and Spirit   17
Chapter 3 'The Face Thing' (Physical Mediumship)   51
Chapter 4 Crystal Working   59
Chapter 5 Working with others   76
Chapter 6 Dreams & Astral Travel   84
Chapter 7 Psychic Abilities   96
Chapter 8 Final bit   105
About The Author   115

Disclaimer - Before reading this book please read the disclaimer

Within this book I have tried to recreate events, localities, and conversations from my memories of them. In order to maintain their anonymity in some instances I have changed the names of individuals and places. I may have changed some identifying characteristics details such as physical properties, occupations and places of residence

Non of the information within this book is intended as a substitute for medical advice and the reader should seek medical advice for matters relating to his or her health particularly with respect to any symptoms that may require diagnosis or medical attention.

The exercises within this book are for entertainment or experimental purposes only. You may experience things which you may not have experienced before. If you feel that you may be vulnerable you should not undertake any of the exercises.

Although the author and publisher have made every effort to ensure that the information in this book was correct at press time, the author and publisher do not assume and herby disclaim any liabilities to any party for any loss, damage or disruption caused by errors or omissions whether such errors or omissions result from negligence, accident or any other cause.

INTRODUCTION

Human beings are miraculous, we are designed to do amazing things for example; we have the ability to use energy and natural resources to heal our bodies and the bodies of others. We can keep in contact with people we love even after they have passed from this world and we can safely astral travel whilst our physical body sleeps. Throughout our time on this planet we are supported by a multitude of Angels, protectors and guides who want to help us, protect us and teach us. All we have to do is welcome them and pay heed to their promptings.

In this book I am going to tell you about some of my lessons in using my incredible human gifts and I will suggest ways in which you too can practice using your fantastic abilities. We are all amazing creators.

Some of us look around our world at our homes, families, relationships, jobs, the multitude of ongoing conflicts sprinkled with occasional triumphs and breakthroughs and we question: Is this all there is? We ride the rollercoaster of life and then get off at the end and that's it? As the late Cilla Black sang in the title song from the 1966 movie Alfie,

> *What's it all about, Alfie?*
> *Is it just for the moment we live?*
> *What's it all about when you sort it out, Alfie?*

Philosophers through the ages have delved into both the objective and subjective aspects of the human being. So broad a notion has been elusive and controversial. Many mystics, prophets and wise folk have shared their insights of being expanding beyond the physical into the spiritual also elusive and controversial. The oft asked question 'What is the meaning of life?' usually leads to more questions than answers, having said that, I keep hearing two answers repeated the first is that life on this planet is the opportunity for our souls to learn lessons and grow the second answer I have heard repeated by many people is that the only thing that matters in life is love and we are here to learn to love everyone and everything and there is nothing else. Personally I think before we work out what we are here for, we should find out what we homo sapiens are and what we are capable of.

In this book I weigh into this discussion by way of personal narrative. Events have guided (pushed) me into unlikely regions where the sceptic in me would never have chosen to go. As a result I have had the opportunity to develop my spiritual self. From an early age I was aware of a spiritual dimension something peculiar beyond the physical. This awareness lay dormant for many years. At times when the spiritual rose through my curtain of doubt – I would push it back or be dissuaded by others from delving into such 'nonsense'.

I am no more spiritual than you are. I do not have any 'spiritual gifts' that you do not have. We are all spiritual beings. As my narrative unfolds, I will share with you some simple exercises which you may find useful in helping to unlock and develop your divine potential.

I believe that when we study spiritual matters and listen to the views of others, we should always carry with us an open mind and a good pinch of salt. An open mind is important because the more we learn about the non-physical world the more beautiful magic we allow into our lives. The pinch of salt is what helps us to be aware that sometimes there is a logical reason for things happening rather than something supernatural. The tap tapping sounds in a house might be caused by a spirit trying to make contact with the living or it might just be water dripping in a radiator pipe. I also believe it is important to recognise that another person's reality is not necessarily your reality. You may find their views and beliefs very strange, bizarre even and, likewise yours to them. Take your scepticism with you when you foray into these interesting realms but do not forget a good dose of respect. As the American musician and band leader Frank Zappa wrote: *"A mind is like a parachute. It doesn't work unless it is open."*

In order for me to progress spiritually to the point I am currently at I have had to experience conflict with others close to me, but my biggest battles have been with myself, my doubt, disbelief and lack of confidence. As I have overcome each hurdle, I have become truer to myself and freer in spirit. However, healthy scepticism that pinch of salt is a good thing to have. There are those on both the earthly and spiritual dimensions only too willing to take advantage of people who are naïve or vulnerable. I hope you will find what I share with you to be a story of hope and inspiration.

In May 2015, I had a conversation with a wise barista aboard a ferry from the Isle of Wight to Southampton in the UK. As he made my coffee, we discussed how insular some people are and how some seem to be afraid to look outside of what they know. The wise barista smiled at me and commented that sometimes, we have to get outside of the bubble before we recognise we are actually living in one. So, be brave, step outside of your bubble and you will discover a whole new wonderful reality. I will not tell you that the spiritual path is an easy one. It presents opportunities which challenge the status quo of your current paradigm. Many people do not wish to venture beyond their comfort zone, and that's okay, we have free choice in these matters. However for those who do wish to learn and develop their knowledge of the spiritual part of our being, the rewards are greater than one can even start to imagine. It is the effort we make in attaining precious things that makes us prize them and the same applies to our stages of spiritual development.

This is my journey over the past few years. I make no claim to having become enlightened and I accept I am still very much 'a work in progress'. Many wonderful events have happened since I chose to embrace my spiritual path. I am only recounting to you what I see as the main thread of my story and some of the experiences I have been blessed with. Many wonderful people have touched my life. Not all will be mentioned herein but I hope that they know I still recognise their part in my growth, and the enrichment they have brought into my life.

The story starts with this book. Three strangers on three separate occasions told me that I should write this book. Each of those people were clairvoyants/mediums and each told me that I should put pen to paper. The message was given at my first and only meeting with each of them. I began writing the book but soon put it down on the premise that I did not have enough time or knowledge to write a book people would want to read.

In addition to the three strangers, a relative nagged me for many years to write. He always said he had a great belief that I would make a mark by writing something and he hoped to produce the artwork for the cover. Sadly I have dragged my feet and he is no longer with us.

The final push came one evening while speaking with my teacher in mediumship, I was told she was being given a very artistic person. I replied it could be one of two people. Her next words were, "You need to put pen to paper." So I did, then I sat on it for another eight years. Then more prompting occurred and I finally finished it. Then I sat on it for another few years before I got round to editing it.
In common with other work I have done, this book has been written under the orders of spirit after much prompting and nagging. Believe me, when spirit decides you should do something, you end up doing it! I sometimes wonder that my guides do not lose all patience with me and leave me to my own devices. I am of course very glad that they do not.

Although I have never knowingly carried out any pagan or witchcraft rituals I have been referred to by family members and friends for most of my life as 'The Witch'. I have no idea why, maybe it is a lack of understanding on their part or maybe it is something I carry in my energy field. It may be of significance that I was born in England in 1951, the year that the 1735 Witchcraft Act was repealed and spiritualists were no longer liable for prosecution unless they fell into the UK Fraudulent Mediums Act 1951 whereby they could be charged for making claims while attempting to deceive and to profit from the deception.

CHAPTER 1 SPIRIT PRODS

I was awaiting the arrival of an External Verifier. The annual auditing visits from an External Verifier was always a bit nerve wracking. External Verifiers (EVs) were employed to audit every activity carried out by training and further education organisations. This ranged from checking on financial transactions to examining the work of a sample of the students as well as interviewing selected students and staff members. In addition to having a full time job I was also a part-time EV myself. Even so, I was always somewhat on tenterhooks myself when my centre was being audited. I knew that no organisation is perfect and a fresh pair of eyes tends to pick up on any deficiencies. I managed a very busy centre where we trained people who worked within the health and social care industry. The EV who was tasked with our audit on this occasion was a person I had not met before. When I was informed by the awarding body that we had a stranger coming my heart sank. As an EV myself I knew that anyone taking over auditing of a centre new to them was going to go through everything with a fine tooth comb. We were in for a grilling.

She arrived exactly on time, a smart looking middle-aged woman with an extremely efficient but not unfriendly air about her. The visit commenced with the usual cup of tea and chat for the woman who's name was Christine to ascertain a base knowledge of how we operated, our students, and turnover of qualifications. She needed to know how many students the centre had, what stage in their studies and assessments they had reached, and if we had experienced any difficulties with providing all the elements required to deliver the qualifications. All of which I was able to easily answer. Then came the scrutiny of our documentation systems. As she worked methodically through the piles of folders in front of her she filled out the standard report form, occasionally asking me questions for clarification but other than that there was little communication. All I could do was sit quietly, supposedly reading and responding to the day's correspondence. What I was actually doing was, running through my head any possible weaknesses in our work whilst attempting to look nonchalant. Completely out of the blue, she laid down her pen and looked very intently at me. My heart sank as I wondered what she had found wrong. She took an ominous deep breath and announced, "I am training to be a medium, and I don't mind telling you".

This really is not the sort of statement one is used to from an External Verifier. I must admit I was totally gobsmacked by this declaration and struggled to find a suitable reply. I came up with something mundane like "Oh that's nice, would you like another cup of tea?" Which was probably not the most dynamic or encouraging of responses, however she smiled at me and continued, "Yes, have you ever thought about becoming a healer?" I do not remember the rest of our conversation except that I know I told her about when I was a military nurse working on the children's ward, whenever we had a critically ill child, I was always called in to work as night special, this was our equivalent to intensive care. It entailed working on a one to one basis with the patient throughout the night. I recalled how I used to sit and watch the children while sending energy to them with my breath. In my naivety I presumed that all nurses did this, and was very surprised after several years to discover this was not the case. I also mentioned to her that I had undertaken a short course in Tai Chi, meditation and healing, and how useful the healing was when friends and family had an ache or pain, especially headaches. Christine told me that I should seriously consider further training as a healer. I was flattered that she thought I was 'special' enough to be a healer (ego popping in I am sorry to say). Nowadays I understand that healers are no more special than anyone else. However, I soon disregarded her suggestion. How could I? A busy professional with a family and household to run where was I going to find more time for further training?

I suspected my husband would be strongly opposed to my involvement in such activity. I was not willing to have that particular battle. I did not see Christine for another three years. Remember, sometimes people flit across our path with one piece of information that can change our life.

Approximately two weeks after Christine's visit, I started teaching an evening course in management studies to a new group of students. During the coffee break, I overheard one of the students telling some of the others of how she often had prophetic dreams. This conversation piqued my interest but my thoughts were on the material I would be covering after the break. Before resuming the lesson, this same student turned to me and asked if I had ever considered becoming a healer. I was very surprised by the suggestion and remarked how strange that she was the second person within a short time to ask me the same question. She assured me that she was certain that it was something I should consider doing. Due to personal issues, this student left the course a couple of weeks later, and I never heard from her again. I am sure she was sent to me as a messenger. By the time I arrived home that evening I had made up my mind that as interesting as this advice from two strangers in two weeks was, I was not going to follow their suggestion I adamantly proclaimed to myself, "Well. I'm not doing it!" I didn't have the time and I wasn't going to battle with my husband over it.

Because my job at that time involved a fair amount of driving around the industrial West Midlands I always had my car radio tuned into a local station to keep up with the traffic reports. Every second week an amazing medium by the name of Vanessa appeared as a guest on one of the morning shows. Whenever I had the opportunity I tuned into the show, I loved listening to her. Listeners were invited to ring in and just give her their first name.

She seemed to tell the caller things that it would really be impossible for someone to guess at. She was always very specific about names, events and messages from their deceased loved ones. I often thought that the people who rang the station were very brave, strangers across the county listening could hear very intimate details of their family life.

About two weeks after the episode with the student, I had to drive from my office to a residential care home not many miles away. As I walked towards my car, the thought went through my mind that Vanessa needed to talk to me. I told myself I was being silly besides; it was not her usual day to be on air. I got into my car and turned on the radio. To my surprise over the airwaves wafted Vanessa's voice! Without thinking I got out of the car, went back into my office and rang the radio station. I honestly believe my actions were not of my own doing, it was as if I were sleep walking. I was told that Vanessa could not take any more telephone calls that morning, and that they were sorry I could not talk to her. I insisted that she needed to speak with me; the female on the other end of the telephone asked me why I thought this to be the case. I explained what had happened and how I had thought that Vanessa needed to speak to me and how I had remembered that it was not her regular day to be on the show and how I had been surprised to hear Vanessa broadcasting. She agreed it was not Vanessa's normal day, and asked me to hold the line for a second. When she came back to me she said she was going to put me through, not to tell anyone else, but I was being slotted in straight away despite other listeners waiting to talk to Vanessa. My heart was thumping like mad, thoughts went through my head like 'please God do not let anyone who knows me be listening' 'Why am I doing this?' and 'what if I am wrong and she has nothing to tell me?' Vanessa asked me to tell her my name. I gave her my official name Elizabeth; this was a rarity at that time, as most people knew me as Beth. She asked me if I was a teacher, to which I replied no. She then asked what I did for a living and I told her I was a trainer. There was a pause, before she asked what I trained, "Dogs?" she asked. I explained I delivered care and management courses. This appeared to amuse her and she pointed out that I was in fact a teacher. She spoke of my looking for a wall clock, which was absolutely true; I had been looking for an antique wall clock, I had even been to specialist clock fairs as well as looking in antique shops. She told me that I would find one, but needed to go to a specialist clock shop. (It took me another two years to find my clock, but I did, however it was in antique shop not a clock shop maybe if I had listened and gone to a specialist shop I would have found one quicker and one that did not stop working as that one did within a couple of years) I was amazed at how accurate she was in knowing I was looking for one, common as wall clocks are, what were the chances of someone ringing in who was actively searching for such an item at that particular time? Vanessa informed me that I would soon be visiting France. 'Oh good a holiday' I thought, I did indeed travel through France not so long after this event, but even more importantly have visited France in a very different way, more of which later. She told me that as well as teaching I was to go on a course myself. As I had not long completed a masters degree, I had no intention of doing any further studying for a while so I thought this unlikely. She then asked me who Mary was, and also who was the lady in the wheelchair with Mary? Adding that the lady in the wheelchair had the same name as me. I knew immediately she was talking of my great, great Aunt Mary who was often with me, in fact she had saved me from a potential car accident a few days earlier and the woman in the wheelchair with the same name as me was Elizabeth, my great, great grandmother and mother to Mary. Then came the bombshell, Vanessa informed me that I was going to study healing. She said, "You are going to come out of the closet". This caused great chuckles of amusement from the gentleman presenting the show, but she pressed on "You are going to come out as a healer". She informed me that Elizabeth was pleased I was going to be a spiritual healer. I felt an enormous wave of emotion envelope me in fact I was so choked with emotion, I could hardly speak, and according to the radio presenter, Vanessa was also feeling extremely emotional! So much so, she was incoherent and he finished the slot thanking her and all of the callers.

Following this astonishing telephone conversation I returned to my car and carried on to the appointment. Lucky for me, the person I was going to see is also a 'sensitive' (someone who is sensitive to the energy of people, places and sometimes entities) She knew as soon as I walked into her office something had happened, and asked me what was wrong. By which time I was totally confused, and to be honest not a little angry that this was being thrust at me. I had long left the nursing profession, I was happily ploughing ahead as a senior manager, besides there was the biggest of all stumbling blocks. I was married to a man who had a great dislike of anything to do with what he saw as paranormal or even a bit 'woo woo'. I was certain that he would resist my becoming involved with spiritual healing. We had been married for nearly 25 years, so I felt certain I knew him well enough to know what his response would be and that I was going to have a battle on my hands if I took that route.

I had learnt at an early stage of our relationship not to mention anything to him that did not fit his paradigm of the 'normal' world. In the early nineteen-seventies before we were married, I was a military nurse and he was employed by the British Army as a civilian ambulance driver. One night we were sat having a drink in the bar when I told him I had to telephone my parents because my great uncle had died. Being a compassionate man he showed concern and asked me when this had happened, he said he was surprised at the news as I had not told him this relative was ill. I replied that the uncle had not been ill; I just 'knew' he had passed over. My then, fiancé gave me a very strange look and insisted on walking with me to the telephone booth in the main reception of the hospital. Although nowadays it is hard to believe, in those days mobile telephones did not exist. My fiancé stood with me whilst I telephoned home. He was able to hear the conversation with my mother:

"Hello Mom"

"Hello Elizabeth, I am glad you rang. I am sorry, but I have some

bad news"
"I know. Uncle Roly has died"
"How did you know that?"
"I just did"
"Of course you did"
My mother then told me the details of the death. As we walked away from the telephone my fiancé who had lost all the colour from his face asked again how I knew, to which I replied again "I just did" How could I explain to him the pain in my heart I always felt when someone passed over, and 'just knowing' happened to me. He looked at me with a taut expression and said firmly "Don't ever do that to me again." He was not the first person to act negatively to my 'knowing'. From then on I knew to keep my mouth shut.

When I undertook a Ti Chi and healing course, I tried to talk to my husband about it, but he made it very clear he did not want to know. When the occasional 'odd' thing happened around me, or if I took away pain from someone in the family and he knew about it, he made cynical remarks about 'the witch'. Under no circumstance would he accept healing for himself from me.

So, here I was, for the third time in a matter of weeks being told to be a healer, not only being told but being told publicly in front of everyone listening to the county BBC radio!

Once we had concluded our work business I sat and talked to my friend 'the sensitive' and cried with anger at being put into this position and said, "I'm not going to do it". My friend was very kind; she listened to my ranting and my concern about what my husband's potential reaction would be. She quietly pointed out that it looked like I was being given a clear message. I understood this perfectly well but had made up my mind that I was definitely not going to listen.

A few days later, whilst I was waiting for my hairstylist to finish dealing with the client before me, I picked up a magazine. I flicked the pages and to my surprise went straight to an article on complimentary therapy. My curiosity was raised so, I read on. Part of the article was about spiritual healing, and at the bottom of the page was the address of the UK National Federation of Spiritual Healers (NFSH). I reached into my handbag and found a pen and piece of paper to write down the address and telephone number whilst inside my head I was still telling myself I was not going to do this.

On 5th February 2000 following urging from several people, the details of which I will not bore the reader with, and, a mini-battle with my husband. I found myself driving to a village hall in the middle of Worcestershire with a packed lunch in a basket and a cushion. I was on my way to Part One of the NFSH training. I was the last to arrive and entered the room with great trepidation. There were approximately twenty other course participants seated in a semi-circle so that we could all see each other. We discovered that the cushion we had been asked to take with us was to ease the discomfort of the obligatory uncomfortable village hall chairs. Anyone who has ever sat on the average English village hall chair for any amount of time will understand why this was such an important piece of equipment. The tutors sat in the gap of the semi-circle behind a low table which was adorned with a bowl of spring flowers, a tea light candle in a container and a plate of small cards, these turned out to be Angel cards. The introductions followed the usual process used at these sort of events, the two tutors showing us the programme for the weekend, introducing themselves, and asking us to introduce ourselves by stating our name and why we wanted to be a healer. As I sat and listened to the other students introduce themselves I felt a huge knot forming in my stomach. It transpired that several students had various experiences of healing as either a healer or a healee, or had undergone various courses of a spiritual nature, and, as to be expected, they all expressed a deep desire to ease the suffering of others. Finally my turn came to speak, I think I managed to get my name out coherently, and probably the name of the town where I lived. Then, to my embarrassment and probably that of everyone else in the room I burst into tears and blubbered that I did not want to be there but had been told I had to attend. My tutors were wonderful, they remained calm and welcomed me with grace.

That weekend we learnt about the history of spiritual healing. It was made very clear to us that we were not expected to work with spirit as in spiritual guides or seeing dead people, but as healers we were to work at soul level with those who requested healing. We learnt about breath and breathing, relaxation, our physical and invisible bodies (otherwise known as the auric field) including our energy centres. The most interesting part of the day for me was the practical session sensing each other's energies with our hands, this was something I had learnt to do on the Tai Chi and healing course, and I loved the sensations. We were led on guided meditations and we practiced the healing act which in this context is healing through balancing the universal life force energy of the individual.

During the weekend one of the tutors mentioned energy bubbles that can be seen all around us. As a child I was aware of these bubbles, and often watched them in the air, I had forgotten all about them and not seen them for many years until couple of days prior to attending the course. I had noticed some whilst driving to work one morning. I was amazed that so soon after seeing them again, they should be mentioned on the course. I was to learn that these synchronicities occur more and more as one opens up to spirit. At the end of the weekend I was pleased that I had attended, but thought I had done enough. When we were departing on the Sunday evening, our tutors passed us application forms for the next part of the course. "Oh no" I told them "Thank you very much, it has been very interesting but I shall not be coming again". The tutor handing the blank form to me smiled and said gently "I'm sure we will see you again next time". She was right, and I kept going back until I had completed all four levels, each time with a minor battle at home, but nothing too dramatic, I am sure my guides and Angels were smoothing the way for me as best they could. The most amazing thing for me during that training was how much I remembered of things I had 'known' or seen as a child, and had forgotten as I grew into adulthood. This remembering was a trend that continued over the next few years. I had of course heard people talk about seeing auras, but previous to undertaking this course did not know what they meant. The delight of realising 'Ah! So THAT'S what I have been looking at around people!' Up until that point and still today, all I see is mainly white, silver or gold, and very occasionally other colours. Of course I sometimes think it would be nice to be able to see a person's auric field in it's entirety but I am sure I am shown what I need to see. I have met people who see the whole auric field and can tell by looking at it exactly where health issues in the physical body have either been or, are currently occurring. Another phenomena I experienced as a child and into early teenage years, which has returned over the last few years, is feeling other people's pain and emotions. From about the age of eight years old, it was not at all unusual for me to develop a headache or pain and within an hour to meet another person with that pain or headache. As soon as I discovered who the other person was who was experiencing the discomfort or pain, I knew mine would disperse, which it always did immediately. I now know, that it is because I am an empath and that I am being given the other person's pain as a message that I should send the person who is in pain healing. It is important to know that the empath should ask spirit to take the pain away from them because a healer's job is to channel healing energy not take the pain from others into our own body. Let's face it, only a crazy person would welcome pain of any sort especially someone else's. A friend of mine once said it is not clever or wise to take on another person's pain or emotional upset and she was right. For that reason it is very important for empaths to protect themselves from other people's 'stuff'. In January 2019 a very mature twelve year old and her mother were sent to see me. The girl was becoming distressed because she was feeling other people's negative emotions, she was astute enough to know it was not her 'stuff,' she also felt symptoms of other people's physical conditions. Thankfully her mother was open minded and the girl herself mature enough, for me to be able to explain to her that she is an empath. Most important of all I was able to give her some suggestions regarding protecting herself. There are suggestions how to do this at the end of this chapter. I was not at fault as a child in not knowing what to do when I experienced other people's pain. It was just part of my learning experience in preparation for the work I was to do as an adult. Of course nowadays I can send healing energy to the person with the pain. But, as a child I did not have that knowledge. I just accepted that I experienced other people's discomfort and it always went away once I identified who it belonged to.

At the end of the final day of the last healing course, one of my tutors asked me what I was going to do to develop my healing skills and how I was going to use them. I responded that I did not know. I knew I still had resistance from my husband to contend with. I also confided to her that having listened to other students I was not sure I was fit to be a healer. All the other students seemed to have been led onto this path of healing through either great sadness or a serious illness, whilst I had always felt I led a rather charmed life. There were of course disasters and crises in my life, but somehow they never seemed to really touch me in a deep way. No matter what happened, things always worked out for the best. Hmmm well maybe I was tempting fate with those thoughts. Not many weeks later THE LUMP appeared in my breast. I had known from when I was in my twenties that one day this would happen. Even though there was no history of breast cancer in my family, it was just a deep seated 'knowingness'. I will never forget the moment when having a shower I discovered it, the cold steel like fear that gripped me, which was followed rapidly by the thought of 'so, at last it has happened' there was almost a feeling of relief mixed in the fear, this may sound bizarre, but I can only recount the truth. Unfortunately many women do not go straight to their doctors, my nurse training however kicked in and I was sitting in my GPs surgery the next day. He was wonderful, he rang the local hospital up immediately whilst I was with him. Although I had to wait fourteen days for the first appointment I knew that the right wheels had been set in motion. As soon as I returned home from that first doctor's appointment I rang my tutors from the healing course they immediately invited me to visit them for a healing session. I knew from that moment on that all would be well. I discovered the lump in May and did not have the operation to remove it until the September. Those four months were the most crucial in my spiritual development, and it was the most amazing of times. It would be dishonest to say I did not have the odd wobble, but I can honestly say I knew I was not going to die of breast cancer. Now as I look back, I thank the Creator for that experience, for without it I would never have met some of my best friends or my main healing guide or experienced such raised senses as I did. I will refer back to this period several times within this book not because it was a morbid time, but because there were several events which would not have occurred had I not had this health scare to deal with.

One of the people who became a very dear friend was a lady called Annie. Annie is a medium and healer. A mutual friend put us in touch with each other and we became firm email pals. After many months we met up for a cup of coffee at a motorway service station. During that first meeting Annie and I discussed healing and mediumship. She told me how certain she was that I was to become a medium. I shared with her my scepticism and I made it quite clear that I had battled with my husband to become a healer and that mediumship was certainly not on my agenda. Like others after her, Annie gently pointed out to me that if Spirit wants you to work for them, you do.

Two years later I was honoured to deliver a course on crystal healing in the School of Spiritual Development that Annie ran in Leicestershire. Annie herself attended the course, if anyone had told me when we first met, that the day would come when I would be teaching Annie anything, I would certainly not have believed them.

I must make it clear that, although my husband always struggled with my interest in spiritual matters and refused any discussion regarding such issues he has always been the kindest of men. Always willing to offer help to others and a magnet to children and animals. Even our daughter's cockatiel which she left with us when she went off to university showed a preference for my husband, chatting to him and squawking if ever he left the house without saying goodbye to it or if he went to bed without saying Goodnight Bea. In my experience children and pets are seldom wrong in their assessment of people. From early on in our relationship I knew that despite living on hospital premises and driving an ambulance he had a fear of hospital wards which was born out of events in his earlier life and yet, he overcame this fear over and over again. When people we knew were hospitalised, he was the first to offer to visit them. A true gentle giant, there is more than one way to be a spiritual person. My husband's path has just been different to mine. I am ashamed to admit it took me many years to truly realise this and appreciate the beauty of his soul.

Try it yourself

>If you are unsure what is meant when we speak of healing energy or a person's energy field (also known as auric energy), try feeling the energy around you. We all have an energy field around us all the time but most people are oblivious to it. The following is a couple simple exercises you might like to try;
>
>**Exercise One**
>Rub your hands together quickly, and then bring them slowly apart. This will help you form a sort of ball between your hands. Move your hands slowly back and forth from each other. People describe what they feel in different ways. My description is, if you could feel fog that is what it would feel like. This is your auric energy.
>
>**Exercise Two**
>Take a few deep breaths, relax.
>Move both of your hands in front of your chest with palms

facing each other. Your palms should be about a foot away from each other and about a foot away from your chest.

Imagine that you are holding a balloon, then try to squish the balloon in a fluid-like motion. As you do this, pay attention to the changes in the atmosphere. Your hands may feel cold, hot or tingly. You may also feel a magnetic force pushing and pulling your hands.

All living things are more than just a lot of cells made into flesh, bones, nerves, skin and bones. As the French paleontologist and philosopher Pierre Teilhard de Chardin said, 'we are not human beings having a spiritual experience. We are spiritual beings having a human experience' Part of that experience might be situations that cause us dis-ease. I truly believe that the majority of illness is caused by factors such as anger and stress. This does NOT mean we should blame ourselves if we become ill because we get stressed or angry judgement is never helpful. There is a difference between true healing and a 'cure'. It is relatively easy to bring in healing energy to cure a headache (or a more serious health condition) be that using allopathic medicine or energy healing. However, if that headache is caused by stress, unless the factors causing the stress are dealt with, the headache will keep recurring or another set of symptoms will appear. Until we deal with the causes of our dis-ease true healing cannot take place. If you or someone you know feel that energy healing will help then I encourage you to try it. However, I cannot stress enough that energy therapy is not a substitute for conventional medical treatment. If someone has a serious health imbalance they should see a Doctor or other appropriate professional, and make complementary healing part of a complete health care programme.

There are many energy healing modalities. You may have already been involved in some of them either as a healee or a healer. If you decide to undertake training as a therapist ensure that you go to a reputable teacher with accredited training that is acceptable to a

relevant insurance company. In the UK there are various sources of information available such as the Federation of Holistic Therapists (http://www.fht.org.uk) and the Reiki Federation (http://www.reikifed.co.uk) amongst others.
I first trained as a spiritual healer with the National Federation of Spiritual Healers in 2000 the word 'spiritual' in this context has no connection with mediumship or the like. In their literature The Healing Trust it is pointed out that the word spiritual originates from the Latin 'spiritus' meaning 'breath of life' (http://www.thehealingtrust.org.uk/)

Since then I have trained in Holistic Crystal Therapy, Reiki and Emotional Freedom Techniques (EFT). EFT has also been known as the 'tapping therapy' however, Gary Craig the founder of EFT has evolved the practice into Optimal EFT which involves working on a spiritual level. He has made a wealth of information available at http://optimal-eft.emofree.com

Protection

Protection from negative energy is important if you are involved in any spiritual practices.There are many ways to protect yourself from other people's energy here are a few suggestions
One of my favourite methods of protection is to imagine myself surrounded by a beautiful bubble or sphere. Just imagine a bubble of light surrounding you from the soles of your feet to the top of your head. Another way of achieving a sphere is to take a deep breath in and as you do so imagine you are breathing up bright white or gold light from the earth and as you breathe out surround yourself with a sphere of that bright light that goes out from the top of your head and cascades all around you. Some people like to imagine zipping themselves up inside a human sized banana skin. I once meet someone who imagined he put on a pair of long johns and then pulled the tops of them right over his head secured with a knot find whatever works for you.

References
(n.d.). Retrieved from http://www.thehealingtrust.org.uk/.

CHAPTER 2 MEETING ANGELS, GUIDES AND SPIRIT

This chapter is an introduction to the subject of angels, guides and spirits I will be talking about them again in later chapters.
I had a very strange encounter in 1968 when I was a 17 years old cadet nurse. At that time, cadets attended college twice a week and were deployed on hospital units for on-the-job experience three days a week. Throughout most of my childhood I always knew I wanted to be a nurse when I grew up. Maybe I was born with a desire to help others, I was certainly influenced by my paternal grandmother who was a retired district nurse and midwife. Although she was retired long before I was born, I remember as a child when we visited the local town near to where she lived she was always addressed by people who knew her with the title of Nurse Charman, never Mrs. Charman. And when her old friends from her nursing days came for tea they always addressed each other as nurse. Hard to believe in this day and age but those long retired women had known each other for at least 40 years and yet, never allowed the familiarity of being on first name terms to creep into their relationships. There was one lady known as Nurse Merryweather (I loved that name) who used to come to tea at my grandparents' house, she and my grandmother had undertaken their nurse training together as young women and yet, the conversation over the tea pot went something like;
"More tea Nurse Merryweather"?

"No thank you Nurse Charman"

Of course this amused a small child, I also remember Nurse Merryweather telling me what a good nurse I was going to make when I grew up, and my little chest used to swell with pride.

So there I was in 1968, seventeen years old and taking my first steps into nursing the only career I ever wanted. The world was my oyster, I should have been happy and care free. However, I was going through a difficult time and suffering a mild form of depression. Often bursting into tears for absolutely no apparent reason. I think my GP put it down to teenage hormonal changes. In addition to the deep sadness, depression and crying I was a normal, difficult, teenager. I think I must have been very difficult to live with. I regularly had arguments with my mother, stepfather and younger sister. On the day of the *strange encounter* I had an argument with someone within the family and flounced out of the house with the intention of walking the mile or so, to a local park. I was good at flouncing in fact I had it down to a fine art along with door slamming. I had almost arrived at the park and, was having a good old indulgent wallow in my thoughts of the unfairness of life when a car drew up alongside me. The driver a fair-haired young man lent over to open the passenger door. Without a thought I got into the car. I may have been a silly and difficult teenager but, to get into a stranger's car was certainly not something I would normally have done. Apart from being far too sensible for such actions, I was quite shy. Nevertheless, without a thought I climbed into the car. I have no idea where we drove to but I do remember that we parked in an elevated position where we could see the countryside laid out in front of us for miles and miles. We just sat and talked. I have no recall of the details of our conversation but I do know we talked about my life and I poured out my troubles to that young stranger. Near the end of the conversation he held out his hand for me to take and made a comment about liking the way I grasped it. He said something about how he knew I had courage from the way I held his hand. He then drove me back to where he had picked me up, there was no discussion about meeting again. I don't think we even exchanged names. It was an odd meeting, an unusual interlude, but the strangest thing of all was according to the clock when I returned home, only a few minutes had passed since I first flounced out of the house! I wish I could remember more details of this incident, maybe I am not supposed to. However, I do recall a wonderful feeling of peace and serenity that surrounded the whole episode.

I promptly forgot all about the car drive with the young man, it went completely out of my head for about 11 years until a time when I hit another low in my life. I was living in Germany, married with a small child and desperately unhappy. One day I sat on the floor in my lounge with my back against the wall and sobbed my heart out. Suddenly the memory of the young man in the car came flooding back, I immediately felt the same deep peace and calmness as I had on that day when I was a teenager. It felt as if he was in the room with me and all my unhappiness melted away instantly.

Not long after the encounter with the fair-haired young man in 1968 a couple of other incidents occurred that should have shown me that I was being watched over. Both of the events involved road traffic accidents I narrowly avoided being in. The first happened when I was out with a friend and her parents one Saturday night. We drove out to a social club some distance from where we lived. There was the usual game of bingo followed by entertainment from a singer. During the evening I developed a headache and nausea. I informed my friend's mother that I felt unwell. She told me that a friend of hers was driving back to the town where we lived and would give me a lift home. I had met this friend a couple of times and he seemed a nice enough man. My mother's friend assured me that I would be perfectly safe in his company and that he would take me straight home. I gathered up my bag and coat in preparation to leave but at the last moment I strongly felt that I aught not to go with him. Even though I still had the headache and nausea I said I felt better and remained until the rest of our party returned home.

Early the following morning my friend came to see me, I was very surprised to see her because I knew she never got up early on Sunday mornings. As soon as I greeted her, she threw her arms around me and started to cry, my mother and I tried to comfort her, we were sure something awful must have happened in her family. It transpired that the man who had offered to give me a lift home the previous night had telephoned her parents that morning to inform them that on the way home from the social club the previous night he had an accident. He had driven off the road on a sharp bend and careered though a hedge. Luckily he was not harmed. However, someone passing by had sent for the emergency services, when the police arrived they had commented on how fortuitous it was that there was not a passenger in the car, they said anyone who had been in the car on the passenger side would have opened the door to get out of the car, and would have fallen to a certain death. The point where the car had left the road was on a very dark country lane on a hill above a very sheer drop. Because of the darkness a passenger could not have seen the drop. Apparently the driver was very shaken up by the thought that he almost did have a passenger. It was the relief that I had refused the lift home and thoughts of what might have happened that caused my friend's tears. I must say I was jolly thankful myself.

My second lucky escape, happened not long afterwards when one afternoon I decided not to board a minibus home from college. Some of the nurse cadets attended the local college but others including me were sent to one in another town about 10 miles away. Two minibuses were provided to transport us to and from the college. The one vehicle picked up and dropped off at the hospital whilst the other drove to the town centre. It was my habit to use the one that picked up and dropped off at the hospital. One lunchtime I kept remarking to my friend Pat that I had a feeling something nasty was going to happen, I could not explain to her why but, I had a horrible feeling high in my stomach. The area which I now know, to be my solar plexus. In those days it was just butterflies in my tummy. Pat quite naturally thought I was being silly and fanciful. However, the feeling persisted no matter how much I tried to push it away and concentrate on my studies. At the end of the day we all made to pile into the mini-buses, as my foot touched the bottom step to board the vehicle a strong little voice said no. I took my foot away and turned to Pat who was stood behind me. I informed her I was going on the second minibus and urged her to do the same. I remember her remonstrating that I always took the hospital bus but I was adamant, she pointed out I would have a long walk home from the town centre, Pat lived-in at the hospital so naturally she refused to take the minibus into town with me. She and I always enjoyed chatting on the drive back from college but nothing was going to get me onto that vehicle.

The following morning was one of my days for working at the hospital. It was my habit to arrive early and have a coffee in the staff canteen before making my way to the department where I was working.

As I entered the canteen a group of my fellow cadets rushed up to me with the news that the minibus I had refused to ride on had been in a collision on the journey back from college.

Luckily none of the cadets or the driver was seriously hurt just a few cuts and bruises. I remember thinking again how lucky I had been.

I have digressed from my story about the young chap in the car on the day I flounced out of the house. But I wanted to give you examples of how messages come to us if we listen there are not necessarily flashing lights and physical manifestations of celestial beings. Sometimes we just need to listen to the gentle inner voice.

In 1999 I again hit an all-time low and felt distressed by life and it's problems, once again I found myself driven to tears, and 32 years after the first meeting, the memory came flooding back again of my fair haired young man who took me for a drive in his car, and again I felt peace, love and serenity surround me as if he were in the room, and my tears just dissolved. I was amazed at how a memory could remove my suffering and as I thought about it I also remembered the time in Germany when thinking of the incident with the fair haired man had also had the same effect on my emotional balance. In that moment I suddenly realised who that young man was. I had met an Angel. And it took me 32 years to realise it! And he had visited me three times in total!

Remember, we never know who we are talking to, so we should treat each stranger as though they are sent from heaven.

I believe angels always come in a form that we can accept ranging from the fair haired young man who I met, to the ten feet high, winged images we see in paintings and church stained glass windows.

Try it yourself

You might find it useful if you or a friend make an audio recording of the following guided visualisation exercises. Some people find it helps to have gentle music playing in the background. If you cannot sit up straight you can still do these exercises but you are far less likely to fall asleep sitting up than if you are lying down. You do not need to sit in a lotus position or hold your hands in any special way, it is important to be comfortable. It is helpful if your feet can touch the floor/ground because touching the floor helps keep us grounded i.e., in touch with our planet. You don't have to close your eyes, some people find it helpful to close their eyes whilst others say they tend to nod off to sleep with eyes shut so instead they prefer to keep their eyes open and use a gentle gaze to focus on an item such as a candle or a spot on the wall or ground. You will find what is right for you. Some people say they are unable to visualise but if in a conversation I mention I have just bought some fantastic shiny, red, high heeled shoes or, a silver sports car I am sure some sort of picture of what I am saying comes to mind. There are a few people who cannot visualise anything at all, including the faces of their nearest and dearest, due to a condition called aphantasia. Aphantasia is very rare. Some people see in technicolour, others sense shape, colour etc. Do not get caught up in having to see everything in minute detail. Whatever you get is right for you. It is also important to note that these activities will be easier some days than others depending on factors such as your mood or, what else is happening in your life, the environment, even the weather conditions can affect our concentration. If you do not feel a session is very successful, do not worry, it will be the next time or, the time after that. If you find your attention wandering and stray thoughts cross your mind such as what else you have to do that day, don't worry and do not try to push those thoughts away, just acknowledge them and let them go. The more we try to push thoughts away the more energy we give them and the more they persist!

Meeting your angel visualisation Exercise 1

Find a time and space where you will not be interrupted. Make sure you are not going to be disturbed by people or phones ringing. It is a good idea to have a glass of water handy.
Make yourself comfortable with your spine as straight as is comfortable for you.
Place your hands in a comfortable position. There is no wrong or right way to hold them. Making yourself comfortable is important, if you are uncomfortable you cannot relax, meditation is about relaxation. Slowing your breathing down is important. When we slow our breathing down we are telling ourselves we are safe. We cannot relax if we don't feel safe.
Check your body from the top of your head to the tips of your toes for any discomfort and resettle yourself for maximum comfort.
Take a couple of good, long, slow, deep breaths.
Imagine yourself inside a protective bubble where nothing can upset or disturb you. Your protective bubble can be any colour you want.
Take another couple of good, long, slow, deep breaths, letting your breaths settle you more now.
Imagine your feet rooted into the earth, you might be able to see lovely golden roots going from your feet deep into Mother Earth.
Concentrate on your breathing for a few moments, breathing in peace and contentment breathing out any worries or concerns that might be bothering you at this moment in time.
Relax and know that you are loved.

As you become more relaxed, more peaceful, more contented, think of a time in your life when you have been really happy, when your heart has been wide open to love.

Capture that feeling, let it soak into your being, become that amazing feeling of love, let that feeling of love wash over you from the top of your head to the tips of your toes.

Let that feeling of love expand out from you and completely fill your bubble that surrounds you, the bubble might also expand. Your bubble might be filled with a pink or white or golden light.

And now that you have made this loving place, invite your angel to step closer so that they are also within the bubble. Wait patiently for them to draw near, and when you know they are close to you, observe them, listen to what they may have to say to you. They might stay for a while or only a fleeting moment.

When it is time for them to go, thank your angel for coming to you and prepare to return to your normal activities knowing you are loved and protected.

Have a good stretch, rub your hands together, wriggle your toes, some people like to stamp their feet a little and have a drink of water.

Meeting your angel visualisation Exercise 2

Find a time and space where you will not be interrupted, make sure you are not going to be disturbed by people or phones ringing. It is a good idea to have a glass of water handy.

Make yourself comfortable with your spine as straight as is comfortable for you.

Place your hands in a comfortable position. There is no wrong or right way to hold them.

Check your body from the top of tour head to the tips of your toes for any discomfort and resettle yourself for maximum comfort.

Take a couple of good, long, slow, deep breaths.

Imagine yourself inside a protective bubble where nothing can upset or disturb you.

Take another couple of good long, slow, deep breaths, letting your breaths settle you more now.

Imagine your feet rooted into the earth, you might be able to see lovely golden roots going from your feet deep into Mother Earth. Concentrate on your breathing for a few moments, breathing in peace and contentment breathing out any worries or concerns that might be bothering you at this moment in time.

Relax and know that you are loved.

Imagine a beautiful warm summer day, you are walking up a quite country lane. Up above the sky is blue with just a few white fluffy clouds, the sun is shining but not too hot, just a perfect heat, birds are singing, butterflies flit from flower to flower along the wayside. This is such a peaceful happy place. You notice a pretty rustic bridge over a crystal clear stream. You walk onto the bridge and look down at the little stream, the sun is golden on the ripples of the water as it meanders over beautiful colourful pebbles, a gentle breeze wafts subtle flower scents towards you, you breathe in the cleansing air full of peace and tranquillity.

You notice a beautiful tree close by with a seat beneath it placed there for you. Take your seat and immerse yourself in this wonderful place. As you sit and absorb this wondrous place you feel the energy of the tree envelope you in it's peaceful loving strength. This is your sacred space, a place where you feel totally safe, secure and protected. Inhale deeply allowing the pure clean air to wash through you cleansing all the cells of your body.

You look up and see the most beautiful rainbow. It seems to be pulsing like a heartbeat of wonderful hues. You are fascinated by this wonderful light show. The colours are bright but subtle and you find yourself surrounded by soothing greens, smoky blues, hazy violets, gentle pinks, they wash around you in tender swirls, it feels so good, so very peaceful.

Close your eyes and allow yourself to be immersed in the colours, allow them to cleanse and purify every bit of you, you might want to spend more time with one particular colour and that is fine too. When you have been washed and purified from the top of your head to the tips of your toes, through your skin and into every organ of your body you notice the rainbow is changing into a golden glow. You are filled with feelings of love and compassion and you see standing right in front of you is your angel. As you look at your angel you have a deep knowing that you are loved and nothing can harm you because you have the loving support of your angel. This angel knows everything there is to know about you and loves you regardless of all you have been and all you will be. No matter what happens this angel will never leave your side. Your Angel radiates pure love and goodness.

Take a little time to talk and listen to your angel. You might like to thank them for being your constant companion. They might talk to you or they might give you something or they might show you something. Just enjoy without judgement whatever passes between you. Take a few moments now to just be. Just be with your angel. (Pause for a few minutes)

It is now time for you to say goodbye, you might like to give your angel a gentle hug then wave goodbye. You notice the waves of rainbow colours are appearing around you both, your angel steps away and merges back into the rainbow. You know there is no need for sadness at parting because you are now aware that your angel is always at your side watching over you.

It is now time to retrace your steps back to the stream and the meadow, everything is as it was before, the birds are singing, the flowers are blooming, the sky is still blue with just a few white fluffy clouds, you make your way back up the country lane and as you do so you notice you feel much lighter and happier than you were at the start of this journey you have an added strength that you never felt before, you almost want to skip and dance your way back. You know that you can come back here any time you want to.

Take a nice deep breath and prepare to be back in the here and now. Open your eyes and be fully present, feeling very alert and ready to continue with your daily life. Have a good stretch, rub your hands together, wriggle your toes, some people like to stamp their feet a little. Have a drink of water.

You might find it useful to make some notes about your journey to re-visit at a later date.

I completed my nurse cadetship and started my nurse training. Halfway through my training aged 19 years old I took myself off into the British Army, where I qualified as a nurse. We underwent our initial training which included such delights as learning how to distinguish one rank from another by stripes on people's arms or 'pips' on their shoulders, how to shine floors so one's face shone in them, how to iron a uniform to perfection and how to march in step with each other. Non of which was of much use to us in our nursing but it served to remind us we were we were now military personnel.

To be honest my intake wasn't very good at marching, in fact so 'not good' that we did not have a passing out parade. It was custom for each intake to have a passing out parade observed by the 'Big Brass', with parents invited to watch and feel proud of their offspring. Not only were we not allowed to have proud parents present to watch us we were told in no uncertain terms that the army was not very proud of us and the Big Brass were not going to be allowed anywhere near us either. We did though, sort of shuffle rather than march our way to a church for a passing out service *without* parents or brass of any kind there to observe our pathetic attempts to stay in formation. We managed to get to the church and back without getting lost. Which is about all one can say about that day. One could say it was not the army's finest hour however, we made history as we were the first (and probably last) QARANC intake not to have a proper passing out parade.

A couple of weeks prior to completing the basic training were told to put in requests for postings and to my delight my request for a posting to Germany was granted. But firstly we had to spend a couple of months in a military hospital in England.

I was sent to Tidworth on the Salisbury planes. During that time in Tidworth a friend and I both saw a person in spirit and we were both very sure she saw us.

The house where I was billeted was an old Victorian one and named after a famous nurse. The ground floor rooms were tiny they had been created by someone wanging up a bit of hardboard and doors to segment large rooms into hutches. The room allotted to me was upstairs and at the far reaches of the building it was arrived at via a series of stairs and narrow corridors and was located next to the washroom. The washroom housed a row of sinks for communal use these sinks were seldom used as most rooms had a wash hand basin and there was no shortage of bathrooms. My bedroom was a spacious airy room and one of the largest in the building, there was a large sash window at either side.

The larger rooms had to be shared by two nurses, I didn't mind this at all because it was better than being in one of the hutches downstairs. Learner nurses were not supposed to be in shared accommodation according to national council rulings. This was because we were supposed to have peace and privacy to study. However, the army was exempt from this ruling for short periods of time i.e. nurses in transit Because some of us were due to go to Germany after a short time we were in 'transit' i.e. not stopping long, we were put into accommodation that was used for those who were just passing through.

On arrival I discovered I was to share with another girl who for the sake of this book we will call Angie. Angie was a pleasant enough person but not someone I would have chosen to be pally with. At the time I thought she was a rather odd-looking girl with her large framed spectacles and flyaway sandy coloured hair that was cut shortish but not in any particular style. It was a wonder that anyone so myopic ever passed the entrance medical into the army. Angie was not very fashionable in her choice of clothes, seeming to have little or no sense of colour. In short Angie unlike my friends and I, did not appear to have any interest in either music, dancing or fashion. Had she been a studious sort of person she would have fallen into a stereotype but I never saw her holding a book and she never shone in the classroom in fact she seemed to struggle somewhat with the academic part of our training. I feel I should point out that at the time I was only nineteen years of age and totally hedonistic in my outlook on life. It was 1970, fashion was exciting and most of my and my friend's wages found its way into the clothes boutiques. There was great music to be danced to and an overabundance of chaps lining up to be danced with. We worked hard and we partied hard. On reflection and with the hindsight that comes with mature age I now see that Angie was a very gentle girl and I suspect a rather lonely one. I am ashamed to say I certainly did not relish sharing a room with poor Angie who was no party girl and I rather regretted the fact that my friend Pam was downstairs in a tiny single room and I was stuck with this oddball of a roommate. However, Angie and I did manage to rub along together even though we never became friends.

One night not long after our arrival in Tidworth I was awoken at 2am by someone entering the bedroom, I opened my eyes as much as I could in my blurry sleepy state and saw someone standing by the door. In the darkness all I could make out was the impression that it was a female (no surprises there, nurses billets were strictly out of bounds to males) and she wore a nurse's outfit with white apron and large white cap the sort that fans out at the back and falls to the top of the shoulders. Army nurses did not wear aprons and learner nurses did not wear large caps. However, I had not long left a civilian hospital where both aprons and large caps were worn and in my sleepy state I did not register the difference between what she wore and the army uniform. I asked her who she was, she did not reply, instead she walked towards my bed, stood over me and smiled, By now I was fully awake and wondering what was going on and why a stranger was in my room. I turned the light on using the pull cord by my bed, as I did so she faded away. It took me a second or so to comprehend what had happened and also to realise that she had in fact walked through both my dressing table and linen bin to stand over me. At that point it also dawned on me that her uniform was out of context. By the time the thought processes had kicked in I was wide-awake and shaking roommate Angie to wake her up. Once she was fully awake and I had repeated to her several times what had transpired, she peered at me in her short sighted way and scolded me that I was being silly and had probably had too many alcoholic drinks before going to bed. I assured her that I had not been near the bar that night and insisted she come downstairs with me to see my friend Pam. There was no way I was going to go down those stairs and corridors on my own. Eventually she conceded and accompanied me. From the corridor outside Pam's room we could see from the light shining through the little pane of glass above the doorframe that Pam still had her light on. I tapped gently on the door and she immediately asked who was there, on being assured it was us she bade us enter. Pam was sat bolt upright in bed, I asked why she was still awake. The story that she told was exactly the one I had come to tell her insomuch she had experienced a visitation the previous night by a 'nurse' wearing an apron and large cap this person had walked through some of her furniture, bent over her and smiled. Angie naturally thought that we had dreamt up an elaborate hoax to tease her. I think she did eventually believe we were not making it up. It transpired that Pam had not told me about her experience for fear of not being believed or my thinking she had just dreamt it. The following day we discovered that some of the men down the road had been playing around with an Ouija board on both of the nights Pam and I had our visitations, we also discovered that in the past nurses had played around with a Ouija board in the house and that on several occasions a child had come though. This led us to wonder if our nurse was in fact a nursemaid rather than a nurse. After much discussion we decided that as she had smiled at us she was friendly and would look after us. We even gave her the nickname Edie because the house was named after, Edith Cavell a famous nurse. Although the military named our quarters after her, one thing is certain, Edith Cavell was never in Tidworth and certainly did not walk around our house at night. Edith Cavell was born in 1865, the daughter of the rector of Swardeston, in Norfolk. After training as a nurse at the London Hospital she became the first matron of the Berkendael Medical Institute in Brussels. After the German Army invaded Belgium in 1914, Berkendael became a Red Cross hospital for wounded soldiers regardless of their nationality. On 5th August 1915, she was arrested by the Germans and charged with having helped about 200 allied soldiers to escape to neutral Holland. Edith was kept in solitary confinement for nine weeks, during which time she was tricked by the Germans into making a confession. Edith Cavell was tried by court-martial, and along with her Belgian accomplice, Philippe Baucq, was found guilty and sentenced to death. She was executed by firing squad on 12th October 1915. I think it was nice that her name was kept alive by the army in naming our house after her.

Pam, Angie and I decided to keep our story from the rest of the girls I think mainly because we did not want to be thought of as being completely potty, but also, as Pam pointed out, we did not want anyone to become afraid of sleeping there for no reason. After all no harm had come to us and neither of us had any subsequent visitations. However, I always had a creepy feeling in the washroom and avoided going in there, instead I went down to the lower floor and used their bathrooms. I also fancied that my bedroom often went cold about 2 O'clock in the morning if I was awake at that time. Of course the chilliness of the building was probably due to it being winter and the army turning the heating down.

Finally the time came for us to depart to our new postings me to Germany, but Pam was to stay in Tidworth for six months and then to be posted to Germany. A couple of days prior to our departure for our new postings, the padre came to give us a talk. When he had finished he asked if we had any questions. With my heart thudding, I raised my arm and told him about the visitations Pam and I had experienced and asked if he believed in such things. To our utter amazement one of the other girls volunteered the information that she had heard of other nurses seeing the same person in their bedrooms. The padre confided that he had heard the same tale several times before. I find it strange that the story of the 'nurse' was not more widely talked about, as nurses were usually keen to talk about the ghosts that roamed whatever hospital they worked in. Most hospitals had a tale of a 'Grey Lady' or a story of the ghost of a nurse from the past attending to or sitting talking with patients in the night, in the morning the patient mentions the nurse who has been exceptionally attentive only to be told that nobody matching that description had been on duty that night.

One thing I am absolutely certain about is the danger of messing with Ouija boards. I was once foolish enough to be involved in using one when I was young, but, in my opinion, people who are not really sure of what they are doing should leave them alone, and those who do think they know what they are doing should also leave it alone. There are many documented stories of bad things happening to inexperienced people during sessions of using the Ouija board.

I went off to my posting in Germany and completed my training. I spent nearly all of my four years of service there with a short break back in England to take my final exams and to spend a few months in a civilian hospital to gain some experience not available in military hospitals.

When I completed my four years' service I stayed on with the army as a civilian nurse.

I discovered a passion for working on the children's ward and spent a total of nearly five years nursing little ones. In-between time I married my German fiancé. Whilst working on the children's ward I had an amazing experience. Having had several days off duty, I was taken on a ward round to be introduced to the children who had been admitted during my absence and to up-date me on the progress of those who were admitted to the ward prior to my being away. The male nurse who was taking me around the patients like most Welshmen in the army was nicknamed Taffy.

We came to one of the baby cubicles where a little boy of about four or five months of age lay. My colleague informed me that this child had been admitted with a chest complaint. I stared at the little one in utter amazement. He was so beautiful and he glowed! He emitted a wonderful golden glow. I asked my colleague to repeat the baby's diagnosis, to which he replied ' a mild chest infection', and turned to leave the room. When I did not follow him he turned back to enquire what was wrong. I could only stand and stare at the child. I clearly remember saying to him 'Look Taffy, he is glowing, he must be very poorly'.
I knew I was looking at the nearest thing to an Angel on earth. Taffy laughed and made a comment like "Oh you and your babies." I was adamant there was something very wrong with that child, and I could not understand why my colleague could not see the light glowing around him.
Within a couple of hours I was sent home to get some sleep because I was required to 'night special' the glowing baby. Night special meant a patient being cared for on a one to one basis and of course there would also be a 'day special' in place. He had taken a turn for the worse and been diagnosed with a severe heart complaint. I nursed him at night for a week or so. The poor little chap had tubes in and out of every orifice and cannulas in his tiny little arms, not once did he cry or look distressed in fact he smiled most of the time. Eventually his condition was stable enough for him to be transported to England to the famous Great Ormond Street Hospital for Sick Children where his little heart was repaired. After a month or so he was sent back to us to continue his treatment. On his return he was still a very beautiful baby but the glow had gone. I have often wondered what sort of man that child grew up to be, and what course his life took, he would now be a man in his 40s.

When my daughter was born in 1976 I decided to leave the children's ward. For a while I worked on the families ward and then on outpatients. I did not feel I could give as much of myself to the children as I had prior to my daughter's birth. Also I did not want to carry infections from the ward back home to my baby.

Not long after I took my daughter home from the maternity hospital I became aware of a presence in our apartment, always around the baby's cot, it took a while for me to realise that this presence was only noticeable when my husband was not at home. He was still employed as a civilian ambulance driver for the army and worked shifts. It took me even longer to understand who the presence was. I am convinced it was my husband's mother. I never saw her although I did see the curtains around the cot move when there was not even a hint of a draft in the flat. I often sensed her and on many occasions observed my daughter looking intently or smiling at something or somebody I could not see. I am sure that my daughter's grandmother was and still is one of her protectors.

I moved back to England in 1979 with my husband and daughter. After living with my parents for a few months, we purchased our first house. It was a small two bed-roomed semi-detached house in a pleasant avenue lined with lime trees. Having lived in a rented apartment in Germany it was wonderful to have a nice big back garden for my daughter to play in and a place to grow a few vegetables and flowers. The gentleman who lived next door was a good neighbour and we soon became friends with him and his lodger. The lodger was a divorced man and father of a large family of children who all came to stay with him at weekends. There were also several other children living in the same street so we had a constant troop of little feet through our house. As is often the way with only children, our daughter seemed to attract every other child in the neighbourhood.

Although it was a happy house and we were delighted to have a place of our own, I never felt the house quite belonged to me. Not long after we moved in I discovered our next-door neighbour had not been friendly with the couple who we purchased the house from, they had only lived there for just over 12 months. However, he had been very fond of the lady who had owned the house before them. He told me how much she had loved the house and how happy he was that we had moved in. He said she would have been pleased that we had bought the house.

My husband worked night shift at a local drop forge factory every second week. One night when he was at work I lay in bed and listened to a clock striking twelve. We did not have a striking clock. I was sure that I had never before heard one next door either, I decided that the neighbour must have purchased one. The following day I was chatting with the neighbour over the back garden fence and asked him if he had a clock that struck on the hour. He looked at me puzzled and assured me he had no such clock. I told him I had heard one the previous night. I then asked him if the lady who had previously lived in the house of whom he had been very fond had owned such a clock, he nodded and said she had indeed. I then surprised him by saying "Ahh yes, and she died in the dining room next to the fireplace didn't she?" The look of surprise on his face was so funny as he stuttered to ask me how I knew that. I just told him I had a 'feeling' about it. With tears in his eyes, he confirmed that indeed she had passed over sitting in a chair next to the fire and he had been the person who found her. No wonder I never felt that house belonged to me. I do not for one minute think that she minded us being in her home and I hope she approved of the improvements we made to the house. We lived there happily for six years but I never quite got over the feeling that it was still her house. Some people do not want to move on once they have passed over. This can be for a variety of reasons including deep attachments to people and places, most do eventually leave but some do remain stuck unfortunately.

I said I would return to the subject of my health scare and as I mentioned earlier not because it was a morbid time, but because there were several events which would not have occurred had I not had this health scare to deal with.

By the time I discovered my breast lump I had a list of people who I sent distance healing to each day and I practiced meditation daily. I have had the honour of having the most wonderful healing guide work with me. To be honest, I think I work with them rather than the other way around. It was during a meditation that I first met Akanawha. I had often heard of people claiming to have a Native American guide. My cynical thought response was always 'Oh yeah, of course you have'. I have since learnt that the reason why so many Native American spirits offer themselves as guides is because of their deep spiritual beliefs and contact with nature whilst on the earth plane. However, as I have already mentioned I used to be deeply cynical of claims regarding such guides. So imagine my surprise when during a meditation session a huge Native American wearing the most amazing rainbow headdress presented himself to me. He did not come alone either but with many other Native Americans, all on horseback. They took me on the most amazing journey. We rode up to a mountain with a massive wooden door built into the side of the mountain itself. The door opened and the others all rode in whilst I was set down and left outside of the mountain doorway. I knew that I was not allowed to follow. I stood and waited on the mountainside until they re-appeared which they did after a short time. I was again gathered up onto the horse ridden by my guide. He then took me to a tent, inside was a lovely woman, it is hard to guess how old she is, but I had a strong feeling of her as a mother. I was laid down and she bathed me and gave me a drink from a bowl. I was shown chamomile flowers. Following this experience I started to drink chamomile tea, something I had previously found unpalatable but now enjoyed. I feel that the door in the mountain I was not allowed to enter was symbolic of the fact I was not to die of breast cancer. Chamomile tea is very calming and was exactly what I needed during that troubled time.

The name I was given for this guide sounds like Akanawha. It took me approximately three years before I was able to find any information that might help explain who he is. I was carrying out some research on the internet into something quite unrelated when I came across a site containing information about a place in America known as Kanawha I learnt that "Kanawha" comes from the Indian name meaning "place of white stone" thought to be due to the salt found in that area. I read that an obscure Indian sub-tribe with a similar sounding name to Kanawha was once located in the area and there was a river of the same name, the Kanawha people are thought to have left the Kanawha River to rejoin the Iroquois people. Which leads me to wonder did I hear him say he was 'Akanawha' or "a Kanawha"? I suspect that names mean far more to us on the earth plane than they do to those in spirit. However, whatever his name, he has appeared to me many times during healing sessions, sometimes he stands and watches me, sometimes he offers advice for instance he said that one woman should have a preparation made from marigolds, sure enough when I researched the subject, marigold cream was just what she needed. I think that marigold cream must be a favourite of his as I have often seen him sprinkling marigold petals over people and in early summer 2004 he insisted that a horse I did some healing on required some of this cream too. A few people have seen him when they have come for healing, just a glimpse but enough to know he is there. I always welcome such sightings as have I frequently doubted that Akanawha exists and told myself I was imagining things because I wanted it to be true. But, he did not give up on me, and kept appearing in my mediation as well as healing sessions. During mediation he has often showed me objects. On one occasion a certain necklace I was shown caught my attention. It had lots of small dark beads, which were fashioned into a lace type design. A couple of weeks later I was trying to locate a supplier of material for my tumbling machine, this is a machine used to polish stones picked up on beaches etc. I looked in the telephone directory and found the telephone number of a shop in a nearby town that sold lapidary items. I rang them up, unfortunately the store did not sell what I was looking for but imagine my surprise and delight to discover that the woman who owned the shop was an old friend who I had not seen for a number of years. I arranged to go and see her. A week later I made the visit and was astounded when looking at the goods for sale to find the exact necklace I had been shown in meditation. It was very beautiful and although I could just about have afforded to purchase it, I did not do so, as I felt I had been taken there just to see it as proof of Akanawha's existence and that he really was with me. What elaborate plans spirit must make at times to catch our attention or to give us reassurance.

Akanawha came to me one July morning during meditation, this time he handed me a multi-faceted crystal. I took the crystal and placed it deep inside of myself. I had no idea what this was about, but thought the crystal very beautiful. All became clear at a later date.

A few days later during meditation I was shown a velvet pad of the sort jewellers use to display their wares, I was then shown items of native American jewellery appearing on the pads. I remember thinking that it reminded me of a market stall. I had no idea why I was being shown such odd items or why I associated them with a market rather than a shop.

Again, I was to find out a while later.

In June I had to attend the hospital for tests. My husband accompanied me and sat outside the consulting room. Poor man, he has a horror of hospitals a hangover from when his mother died, he was only a teenager when he she passed over. I donned the obligatory paper gown and sat on the bed for what seemed ages. I told myself I would be fine, a little ripple of panic rose in me. What if I were wrong? What if it was really bad news? Suddenly, I had the sensation of something being placed on my head, although not very heavy it did have weight, slowly it dawned on me what it was. My guide had placed his headdress on my head! All the fear subsided immediately. After I had been seen by the specialist, and had been prodded and poked, my breast ironed by the mammogram machine and samples taken, I had to go the reception desk to make my next appointment. The outpatient department was in a modern building with the consulting rooms built along the walls in a square and the waiting areas and reception desk in the middle. The consulting rooms had windows, but the waiting and reception areas had no natural light at all. I stood in the queue waiting for a clerk to deal with me, my husband besides me. Suddenly I heard the sound of wind chimes. I looked around to see where they were. I knew that the consulting rooms did not have buzzers, each patient being ushered in by a nurse who called out the patients name and showed them which room to go in. There were no windows and no drafts to ring a chime. I looked at the receptionist and smiled, I was just about to ask her where the chimes were when something stopped me speaking. Once we were outside I asked my husband if he had heard the chimes. Of course he had not, it was my dear guides giving me a little tinkle to tell me not to worry.

On the 14th August 2000 I wrote in my special diary:
Today I went to the hospital again. I am to have the lump removed from my left breast on 15th September – day care case and have been advised not to book any work for the following week. I am not worried about this lump at all. I woke up in the night with raging toothache in my lower right jaw. I think I must have been clenching my teeth during the night, perhaps I was a little bit worried after all.

 During my morning meditation I saw my Native American's headdress again, it was long right down his back and still rainbow coloured. I was given crystal balls again (I am often given crystal balls). This time not multi-faceted but clear, one had a rose colour in it, (later when I trained as a holistic crystal therapist I learnt that this was rose quartz the crystal of Universal love) *I felt very emotional at the sight of him and the crystals. He rode to a cave in a high cliff again. I had the choice this time to enter or stay out. I said in thought If this is death I do not want to go in, if it is enlightenment I do. I stayed outside. I then saw hundreds of Native American Women holding hands in a very long line against a background of red rock. I was shown that I am at the top of the high cliffs and can fly.* I have discovered through conversations with Native American friends that to see these women in mediation is not so unusual. They are the infinite ones, the grandmothers. I can still remember what they looked like, each wrapped in a shawl, and I still recall the wonderful sensation I had of being part of them

Whilst I was in the consulting room at the hospital sitting waiting for the doctor to come I 'saw' I was being propelled rapidly down long corridors and through square doorways. I was worried the doctor would come in before I was finished traveling to wherever my guides were taking me, I suddenly saw beams of light surrounding me and I was okay.

I had completely forgotten about the vision of the corridors until I came to re-read my diary for the purpose of writing this book. I can only presume that the being propelled down corridors was my guides taking me through a time passage.

Prior to my operation, my guide informed me he was going to ask his people to sing and dance for me for a night and a day, and I believed him.

Now reader, you would be fully justified in thinking that someone faced with the prospect of an awful illness or disease may well look to other realms for help support and guidance, and maybe become slightly 'unhinged' within the process. I can assure you that it crossed my own mind that this might be the situation. But, I had witness that this was certainly not the case. A week or so after my operation a friend who has been aware of spirit most of her life but, does not often use her gifts, came to see me. At this point she did not know I had undergone the operation, nor was she aware of my guide. During the week in which I had the operation, she and her family were on holiday in Scotland. She told me that one day whilst they were on their Scottish trip they were driving along in their rented camper van, when suddenly she heard Native American chanting, she could not work out where it was coming from. She mentioned it to her husband who thought she was imagining it and told her in no uncertain terms she was going 'batty'. It transpired that the day she heard the chanting was the day before I had my operation, during the period when I was told they would sing and dance for me.

Several people have been lucky enough to see Akanawha during healing sessions, usually people who do not believe in guides and such like. I think he shows himself in such situations to help the individuals with healing their spirit as well as their body. It is wonderful to see the look of surprise on someone's face when they glimpse him stood behind me. One such person was a friend of my husbands. For the sake of privacy I will call him John. John had a continual persistent cough. One night I went to collect my husband from a bowling green club both he and John belonged to. John was there and persistently coughing. My husband asked if I thought a session with my sister might help his friend John to stop coughing. My sister is trained in massage, reflexology and aromatherapy. I replied that I did not know if my sister could help or not but if his friend would allow me to, maybe I could channel him some healing. John agreed. We went into a small room no larger than a cupboard. Once ensconced with the door shut firmly between us and the other club members, John informed me he did not know what all this 'healing stuff' was about but would give it a try. He also stressed that he did not believe in 'anything'. On questioning it turned out he was telling me he did not believe in God, spirit or any of 'that stuff'. He declared vehemently that when you die, you die, and that's it. I accepted his views and explained that healing was about working with vibrating energy. When I scanned his body I found a weakness in the throat area and another in the lower bowel. This amazed him; he told me that he felt his cough problem was in his throat although his doctor kept treating him for a chest complaint. Also he did have lower bowel problems, which he had not discussed with his doctor or anyone else. I think the fact that I had felt these two areas of weakness gave him a little trust in me. Following that evening, I did not see John for several weeks, when we did happen to meet again he informed me that he had not coughed at all for days after seeing me, but the persistent cough had now returned. Then he added that it had stopped the moment I had walked into the room. John agreed to come and see me in my home for another healing session. It soon became clear to me that John's cough was stress related, and he agreed that this was the case. He became a weekly visitor to my healing room for many months, not because he needed the healing because the stress and therefore the cough were under control, but because he became so fascinated by things of a spiritual nature, not to mention loving the 'trips' he took during the healing sessions. On one occasion during one of his early visits we were sat chatting about his experience during the healing when he suddenly stopped talking and looked at me opened mouthed. I asked him what was wrong. He could hardly stammer out the words that he had seen an 'Indian' stood behind me. I asked him to describe what he saw; sure enough he had seen Akanawha. We had many spirit people pop in to visit us during John's visits, including his grandparents and great grandparents. On one occasion whilst working with John I was shown a boy in an old-fashioned hospital bed with a nurse in a long uniform stood beside him. I was also shown a woman and a tin box, and within the box was a photograph. When I told John what I had seen he had no idea who the boy in the bed was and denied any knowledge of such a box. I asked him to look out for the box. A couple of weeks later John arrived in my healing room grasping a tin box. He had travelled up north to visit his mother who had given him the box containing various old documents on top of which was a photograph of the woman I had described to him. Also, come into his possession was a photo of his uncle taken when he was a boy in hospital, hence the old-fashioned hospital bed. John's views on life and death did a complete turnaround; he borrowed books from me on a variety of spiritual topics and now has a healthy interest in things of a spiritual nature. Having opened up his mind he is now aware of spirit and has had some very interesting experiences on his own. He even sat in my spiritual development circle although it did take him fifteen years to get around to that.

It is absolutely not essential for healers (or those who come for healing) to be interested in the spirit world. I know excellent healers who are not at all in touch with the spirit world, in the sense of working with people who have passed into spirit. Such healers are of course working on a spiritual level with their clients. Communicating with people who have passed into the spiritual world has become very much part of what I do. I find that people who come for healing are a mix of those who are aware of the spiritual realm and those who do not believe in spirit. So, my healing is often dual purpose, to help deal with the condition they present to me and to put people in touch with the spiritual world. I do not believe it would be right to try to persuade people to follow my belief system and I certainly do not try to ram spirit and God down their throats. In fact it is rarely me who raises these issues but somehow clients seem to end up saying something that starts the conversation going or as is more often the case something happens during the session that opens up their awareness. It is not unusual for them to have a spiritual experience during the healing session such as what happened with John. Another example of this was a woman who came for healing for a persistent back problem. As is so often the case, by the time she came to see me, she had already made numerous visits to her general practitioner, had several sessions of physiotherapy and spent a large amount of money on treatment from an osteopath. Of course these people are all professionals and they do an excellent job. However, I do find it sad that a lot of people visit a healer as a last resort, instead of seeing healing as complimentary to mainstream medicine and visiting a healer from the outset in order for the healer and others to work together. When the woman who we will call Mary, first arrived at my doorstep, she was doubled up in pain and walking like a ninety year old, she was in fact only 45 years old. The first thing I did was to ask Mary to sit on my ergonomic stool, this was not magic, and not healing as such, but the look of relief on her face as the pain subsided just because she was in a position that relieved the pain. Healers have to use common sense as well as working with energy and as she relaxed on the ergonomic stool it was much easier to carry out the healing session than if she had been uncomfortable or in pain. Mary visited once a week for several months, like John she returned many times after the back pain was healed. Over a period of weeks I worked on her chakras, performed laying on of stones and did some meridian clearance. After a couple of visits her deceased grandfather and aunt started to pop in with little messages. Mary's grandfather also started to make his presence felt in her own home, she and other members of her family sensed him and smelt his pipe tobacco. The family found his presence very comforting and did not even mind him smoking in the house. Her aunt was lovely and we laughed the night she gave me a message to tell her niece to make sure she dried her hands properly with the warning 'You don't want to end up with hands like mine'. What I did not know until this event was that Mary did indeed have a habit of washing her hands and not drying them, her aunt had suffered from very bad arthritis's in her hands, so was giving a timely warning. Mary told me that prior to visiting me she had a vague belief in spirit but had always been rather scared by the thought of ghosts. There was another spin-off from Mary's visits. Healers are very aware that much of the pain, discomfort and illness experienced by people are due to dis-ease. This dis-ease can be caused by many things for example unhappiness in one's job, environment, or relationships. Some people also believe that we bring certain conditions into the world with us from past life injuries. Mary was very unhappy in many aspects of her life, so the visits she made to me were also counselling sessions. I feel that it is very important that complimentary therapists not only train in their healing modality but I think that they should also be formally trained in at least basic counselling techniques.

One night Mary rang and asked if her daughter could take up her next appointment instead of her, naturally I agreed.

The daughter who we will call Susan had a painful knee. Prior to starting work on a new client, I like to scan their aura using my hands. This involves moving my hands around the body from top of the head to the tips of the toes, front and back, and down the sides; I tend to hold my hands approximately a foot away from the physical body. It is my understanding that different healers feel different sensations when scanning in this way, but, for me, if there is an area that requires particular attention healing or, balancing it feels as if there is a cold spot in the aura, sometimes it almost feels like a cold breath on my hand in the affected area. I located such a cold spot around this young woman's sinuses. I mentioned to her that I thought she had either had in the past or, presently had a problem in this area. As I recall she neither confirmed nor denied that she had a sinus problem. I worked on her knees with my crystals and, at the end of the session she asked, if she might return the following week so a further appointment was booked. The night before her second appointment I had a very strange dream, which made no sense to me at all at the time. I was shown a number of flat stones laid out in a square, there were pictures or patterns on the stones but I do not recall what they were, a voice bade me to choose a stone I took one from the bottom right hand corner and the voice which had asked me to choose a stone said "Elizabeth, this is your family you are Hopi" When I awoke and remembered the dream I wondered what a 'Hopi' was? When Susan came for her healing session we entered into the customary chat about how she had felt since the last session. I was totally surprised when she reminded me that on the first visit I had mentioned a problem with her sinuses. As she had not reacted to my comment I had let it go. She then told me that she did indeed have a problem in that area and that earlier in the day of this second visit she had, visited a therapist for Hopi ear candle treatment. As she told me I felt a great thud in my solar plexus and sensed someone in spirit having a laugh at my amazement. At that time, I had no idea what Hopi ear candles were, this was some years ago, of course candle treatment is more widely known about nowadays in the UK. Naturally I tried to find information regarding the Hopi Indians but found nothing that could explain my strange dream, it was not for a couple of years that I was to be given any further information that would shed any light on the matter. The explanation is given later in this book. The point of this story is healing and working is not a one way process with all the information and support going to the healee. The healer also receives information and support

I do not consider myself a working medium as I do not do sittings for a living, however I do occasionally pass on messages from the other side outside of my healing work. A young man who worked for the same organisation as me had a grandmother who passed over. He was telling me about his loss and I kept getting a picture of a very odd box, in the end I described the box to him. To his delight he was able to identify it with his grandmother, it was something that meant a great deal to him and her. On another occasion I was chatting to a colleague when I kept getting a picture of a necklace, imagine my surprise when I described the necklace to her and she drew it out of her handbag. It was an item that had belonged to her late mother. As I held the necklace I saw her mother wearing her favourite outfit and then was shown many items that had belonged to her. The daughter was delighted and realised that her mother was still close by. At times like this I wish I could draw, because my hands wave around in the air as I try to express the shape of things and I have to use words to describe what I am seeing. Finally, I asked the colleague why she had not sorted out her attic because her mother kept showing me items that had belonged to the daughter and were now stored in the attic. The colleague looked at me in surprise and informed me that she and her husband had been talking about doing exactly that. What she did not tell me was that they were planning to move house which they did a couple of weeks later. No wonder I kept being shown some official looking documents as I drove away that day. During the same session I was repeatedly shown tables set out with white tablecloths and napkins and floral arrangements. When I told her about this she laughed, her son unknown to me had got married a couple of weeks earlier, of course her mother was just letting us know she was at the wedding.

I will admit that at times it can be daunting to tell someone that you have a message from spirit, especially when you know the person well but they have no idea of your clairvoyance. If the message you are given is going to help them that is a small price to pay for a little embarrassment.

Around the same time as Akanawha came into my life, so too did Ishmael. To me he appears as a gentleman from India although, one very good medium once told me he is from Turkey. He made his first entrance during a meditation session. What a shock I had when the day following the meditation when he made his first entrance, a friend told me she had seen a gentleman from India standing beside me, she described exactly the same clothes as I had seen him wearing including, the gold turban. Ishmael often shows me items, I am sorry to say that sometimes it can take a very long time for me to work out what these items are and what they are to be used for. Sometimes he does speak to me but then it is often in riddles and again it can take me a long time to work out the meaning of the riddle. It is Ishmael who prompts me to carry on in difficult times, giving gentle reassurance that I am on the right track.

For a while, Ishmael was accompanied by a young boy by the name of Barnabas who said very little in fact he was so quiet I often forgot he was there. I remember on one occasion in late spring of 2004 I had lunch with a friend. The friend is a medium she told me that a spirit child resided in her house, a pretty little girl from the Victorian era. Although my friend is a medium it was her husband who saw the child, my friend sensed that her husband rather liked seeing the little one. On the first occasion she told me about the child I commented how the little girl needed to go home as there would be family waiting for her, I also asked her if she knew the child's name she did not, so I asked her to request her husband to ask the girl her name. The next time we met she reported that she had indeed asked her husband try to find out the name of the little girl and that the very next time he saw her she had her name embroidered on her apron top, my friend also told me that she had told her husband to let the little girl know it was time to go into the Light and he said he had. However, my friend sensed the child was still in the house so I was invited over to the house for lunch and if possible to investigate into what was happening with the little girl. On the drive to my friend's house I became aware that Barnabas was with me, on this occasion instead of his normal eastern outfit he wore a shirt and shorts, and he informed me that he was coming with me that day with the quest of taking the little girl home. It was the first time I had visited the house. Whenever we met up it was at either her or my workplace, so I had no idea of what the interior looked like but, no sooner than I got there than I had the impression of the little girl sitting in front of a pine wardrobe playing with some toys. I asked my friend if she had such a piece of furniture and why I saw the child there. My friend laughed out loud and informed me that her youngest son was the only person with a wardrobe that fitted the description and he kept a pile of toys in front of it. We sat out in the garden as it was one those rare hot sunny days we sometimes get in England in the month of May, we drank coffee and enjoyed each other's company. As my friend and I chatted about this and that, I gradually became aware that the little girl and Barnabas were playing on the lawn. I turned and watched as Barnabas took her by the hand and led her in a slightly upward direction where a lane appeared and a youngish woman dressed in brown walked towards them. I felt very privileged to watch the joyful reunion between mother and child and inwardly thanked Barnabas for his work. On reflection it is strange that I did not tell my friend what I had witnessed even though I had told her on my arrival at her house that Barnabas was with me and would take the child home but for some reason I just watched the proceeding and kept silent. A couple of weeks later I rang my friend and asked her if she sensed the child was still in the house and to tell her of the daughter and mother reunion I had observed. She reported that not only did the child appear to have gone but that her small son seemed to be much calmer. She went on to tell me that she had recounted to her husband how I had visited for lunch and how Barnabas had accompanied me with the view to taking the little girl home. She also told him what I had said about the wardrobe and toys. Apparently her husband had looked shocked at this, and then confided in her that when he tucked him into bed at night, their son had been for some time asking him to turn his teddy bears which were kept by the wardrobe so they faced away from him because 'they looked at him' but since Barnabas and I had visited this ritual had stopped. My friend and I could only surmise that the boy had sensed the little girl looking at him as she sat with the toys. It is a wonder that her son did not see the little girl because children are often very open to spirit. Not long after the visit to my friend's house Barnabas disappeared. This does happen with spirit, sometimes we have a guide work with us for years and then suddenly they go. No goodbyes, they just go. This can be a bit upsetting because as with physical people we get fond of them. The fact is that their job is done and they leave.

I think we may have more guides with us than we are aware of. I have been told on several occasions by mediums that I have with me a Chinese man and a nun, the Chinese man did not show himself to me until I became a Reiki Master, I still haven't seen the nun. I believe different guides come in at appropriate times to help us with specific situations or to help us develop certain gifts, when the time is right. We must of course be willing to open ourselves to such help. There are many different methods espoused by teachers in spiritual matters for contacting spirit guides, I feel people should explore a variety of techniques and find the one that is right for them. I have been lucky, as my guides have made themselves known to me in gentle ways which have felt perfectly natural to me.

In June 2003 I was working on a young man who came for healing for a heart condition. Near the end of the session I saw standing in front of me a very handsome Native American man. I will never forget the feeling of seeing him standing there, it was pure joy and love and as if I was being reunited with someone very dear after a long separation. Although, I had never seen him before, I just knew him. Apart from his beautiful face the detail that caught my eye immediately was his hairstyle, one side was plaited the other hanging free. He came, looked at me and went.

Afterwards when I reflected on the event I wondered if he had come with the young man I was working on healing rather than coming to see me. I have to admit I was rather perturbed at this thought. A few days later he appeared again, this time sitting beside me whilst I drove to work. So I took the opportunity to ask his name and was given 'Standing Bear', my sceptical self, kicked in and I thought 'Oh yeah, of course, just like in the cowboy films'. However, I thought about him over the next few days and finally decided to do an Internet search to see if I could find anyone documented by that name, sure enough I did, and what was even more amazing I found a photograph. There he was wearing his hair in exactly the same style as I had seen! I was truly amazed at this. Of course I wondered if I had seen this picture before, maybe by accident whilst browsing for something else. Maybe I had imagined him.

Standing Bear continued to come and go, he never spoke to me or showed me objects as other guides had, neither did he appear to help in the healing work. What I did feel when I saw him was the most amazing feeling of strength, and I felt that he came to give me strength to do my work. Then one day I saw him holding a lifeless form, he appeared to be standing on a cliff top and looked distraught, this happened several times. Then came the occasion when he held the lifeless body in outstretched arms towards me, as if offering this body to me. I instinctively knew it was his daughter but could not understand the gesture, until one night I mentioned it to the medium development circle I sat in. One of the other mediums said immediately that I should accept the gift of his daughter he was offering me and what an honour that he should make this offering. I was unsure, as I did not know what I should do with the body, I was assured that he was giving me the greatest gift he could and that I should take her. So the next occasion when I saw him and he offered her to me I told him I would accept his daughter. I have discovered that Standing Bear's adult daughter died on the trail of tears on 5th June 1877 the cause of her death was tuberculosis.

CHAPTER 3 'THE FACE THING' (PHYSICAL MEDIUMSHIP)

After I told him I would accept his daughter, Standing Bear did not make another appearance for several weeks, but when he did it was rather spectacular. I was at work sitting in a meeting room talking to a colleague, suddenly she looked rather puzzled and informed me that I had a white stripe across my cheekbones and nose, then another appeared across my forehead, thinking I could brush whatever it was away I rubbed my face with my hands. My colleague told me to stop what I was doing and sit still. She then gave me a running commentary about what was happening to me, a feather appeared in my normally blonde hair which had now turned very dark, my eyes also changed from green to brown and apparently I looked like a man. If I recall clearly her exact words were "If I did not know better, I would believe you are an American Indian".

Whilst all of this was happening I had the sensation of looking at the colleague as if she was a long, long way away. I could hear her words and see her but was not able to move, I did not feel as if I was becoming another person even though the description of my face was far removed from how I see myself in the mirror. I did not feel afraid and neither did my Colleague which is odd, because I am pretty sure if I watched someone's face change into another person I would be totally freaked out.

The whole episode took approximately three to four minutes, of

course we chatted excitedly about it afterwards. My colleague wanting to make sure I understood what she had seen. I asked her if she would recognise him again, she was definite that she would so I logged onto the Internet and found a picture of Standing Bear, she took one look and without hesitation declared "That's him!"
Naturally we both wondered why he had appeared in that way, for he could surely have just stood beside me and made his presence felt and seen. Several days later I recalled a conversation I had with another friend who is a medium, she had told me that she thought I would be doing some physical mediumship in the near future, and as usual, at the time I had thought Oh yeah, of course I am (not).
I tentatively started to work with this phenomenon by practising with people who I knew well and trusted, people like myself who were sensitives, people I trusted not to discuss what I was doing with others. We had some amazing experiences. The range of faces that were seen males, females every skin and hair colour imaginable, fascinated me.
On one occasion the woman who had first seen Standing Bear asked me if we could do 'the face thing', we had by then had several of these sessions and I felt we worked well together. I believe the other person has to be receptive and willing to look at whatever or whoever appears with an open mind. I have to trust that person to behave in an appropriate manner and respect spirit.
On this occasion my friend and colleague reported seeing several faces including a Native American Elder, suddenly she reported that I had a picture of a tree on my forehead. A second before she reported seeing the tree, I heard a voice in my head saying
"See all knowledge see ancient wisdom" the woman I was working with was sure that the tree had some specific meaning but did not know what. We took a break and tried again. The tree re-appeared immediately. I was instructed to ask her to look at the wall behind me as she moved her gaze from me to the wall I heard 'Now she see, now she understand' apparently the tree had reappeared behind me but was now clearer to see and was a silver birch tree, however, she still did not understand why she was

being shown it. I was instructed to ask her to move her attention back to my face, as she did so I heard a voice say just two words "Fear not". I knew she was seeing something but was not telling me what she was looking at. I managed to ask her what she was looking at, I should add that I find speaking rather difficult in this altered state. My friend said she was looking at a Native American but she had seen something before and would tell me about it later. I immediately knew instinctively what she had seen. I was then given more instructions the voice was very gentle but very authoritative "Daughter of Standing Bear stand" I stood up "Daughter of Standing Bear" stand by chair. I knew I was to move to the right of the armchair. As I did I heard "Now big people come" I moved my focus back to my friend and saw absolute awe on her face.

Minutes later I was back in my seat and asking my friend what she had seen before the Elder appeared, she looked rather embarrassed and said she thought I would think her completely mad if she told me. I reassured her I certainly would not, and I thought I knew who she had seen anyway. She described having seen the most amazing brightest golden halo around my head then looking straight into my eyes quietly murmured "I saw the face of Jesus" her declaration came as no surprise, however, I am still not sure if the "Fear not" message was for her or me. I then went on to ask what she had seen when I stood up and when she recounted what she had seen the message 'Now big people come' made perfect sense. She had seen a massive golden winged being although the details, for example, facial features were not clear she was certain she had seen an angel.

We naturally spent some time discussing these events and agreeing that we were not going to tell anyone what had transpired as we were certain people would think us both completely mad. It was during this conversation she suddenly asked me if we could do an internet web search for silver birch. As we were both originally country girls and very capable of identifying what a silver birch tree looks like and where they grow I thought this an odd request but then my friend explained she was sure that there was a book called The Teachings of Silver Birch and that she had been given a copy a year or so beforehand but had never read it. We carried out a search on the Internet and sure enough we discovered that Silver Birch is said to be an evolved spiritual being who, returned to what he referred to as 'the world of matter' in the guise of an American Indian Spirit He channelled through an English trance medium by the name of Maurice Barbenell, in England, for over 60 years and indeed, as my friend said there is a book titled The Teachings Of Silver Birch. Having since done a little more research on this spirit guide I now understand why, when he appeared to my friend I heard 'see all knowledge see ancient wisdom'. On another occasion when I worked with my friend she informed me she was looking at a Native American elder, I remember looking at her and knowing she was thinking that I (he the elder) was looking right into her soul, she saw several other people during the session. When we were talking about it later she said to me "I had the oddest sensation when that Native American looked at me, do you know what it was like?" I replied that I thought she felt her soul was being searched, she affirmed that this was indeed exactly what she thought and furthermore she knew that I knew that was what she was thinking. She found it rather disconcerting to be so scrutinised. So would I if I was in her shoes!

The sceptic might wonder why such amazing ascended masters such as Jesus or Silver Birch should bother working with two nobodies such as my friend and I. Well, if we work on the presumption that it is correct to say we are all equal in the eyes of God, why should they not work with us? We are no more special than anyone else, but, maybe we are no less worthy than anyone else. Maybe at that moment in time we needed the support of these special spirits and maybe we were open to them. I would urge anyone wishing to consider the meaning of spirituality to read *The Teachings of Silver Birch.*

I think the 'face thing' could be very disconcerting for anyone if they were not expecting to see someone they knew who has passed over. No matter whether they were on good terms with that person at the time of their passing or not. However, the people I have worked with to-date have always appeared to take it in their stride. Even when they have initially been surprised or amazed at what they have seen. Not everyone is willing to talk about what they see and that has to be respected. One morning at work I was asked to speak on the telephone with a mature student nurse who was having a tough time coming to terms with events in her life. I was immediately contacted by her grandmother, later I discovered that this grandmother had only passed over ten weeks prior to my speaking with her granddaughter. The deceased woman was desperate for me to tell her granddaughter how sorry she was about traumatic events in her granddaughter's life she (the grandmother) had done nothing to stop happening and she had to some degree denied that they had happened and had covered them up. At her request, I met up with the student nurse a week or two later. We worked together with me doing the 'face thing'. Afterwards she said she was pleased we had met up but she would not tell me what she had seen, only that it was a very emotional experience.

After a period of time my guides found ways of letting me know when they wanted me to work with them. For a while they gave me or the person who needed a reading the smell of wood smoke, the smell of camp fires. This happened on one occasion when I was talking to a colleague. She suddenly informed me that she could smell wood smoke; as soon as she uttered the words I had an idea that this was the reason. I made some remark about not being able to smell anything myself which was true. We moved around the building during the course of our conversation, three times the colleague mentioned the smell each time I asked her to move a few feet away from where she stood and asked if she could still smell it. Each time the response was the same, she could not smell the smoke when she moved, but when she moved back it would be still there. Finally I told her I thought I knew what it was all about and asked her to sit opposite me at the board table in the meeting room. I knew that it would be okay to work with her, she occasionally used the tarot cards herself and had on several occasions mentioned to me that her mother was a seventh child of a seventh child and very psychic although she chose not to use her own psychic gifts often. It was lunchtime so I felt it was okay to deviate from the reason she had come to see me and listen to spirit.

It did not take many seconds for me to tune in and the 'face thing' happened, the colleague's great aunt who was in spirit appeared in my place. She told me of a time when the colleague was a child and a funny event that took place, this made my friend laugh. After a short period of time the great aunt was replaced by my colleagues father who was also in spirit, he wanted to apologise for the way he had treated his daughter and my hand went to the kidney area of my back. The colleague barely managed to utter the words "That's where he used to hit me". He apologised again. After the session we chatted about what had occurred until I felt a cold feeling down my back and was nagged by the great aunt. She showed me in some detail my colleague's front garden how it had been when she had moved into the house barely 12 months earlier, she even took the pains to show me specific plants and where they grew. She then showed me the inside of the house, articles of furniture, crockery, décor all in detail. She was of course wanting to let my colleague know that she popped in now and again to see what was going on. This was not just a matter of a spirit wanting to give witness of the spirit world and how they are still with us, she had a message for the colleague which included a warning of something the colleague's son wanted to do. He owned a small motor scooter but was going to ask for a big motorbike, the aunt did not think it would be a good idea. One week later I saw my colleague again, she told me that during the intervening weekend the son had indeed asked for a big motorbike, my colleague and her husband had said no. Although I think on this occasion the advice was good and probably best heeded, I do tell people that if they would not have trusted the advice of a person when they were on the earth plain, there is no good reason to trust that advice once they have passed over. I have sat in spiritual churches where the medium has given messages from departed relatives such as saying they don't like the wallpaper their relative has used in their lounge, or their new hairstyle followed by the suggestion they change the hairstyle back or re-paint the lounge. And, I have watched the relative sit in church and nod their head as if they are going to take that advice. Why? If you did not take granny's advice on your haircut when she was here on the earth why would you listen now? Just because somebody has passed over does not make them the fountain of all knowledge. But if you trusted their judgement when they were here, trust it now, but, be absolutely sure that you are certain it is coming from them and not from the medium or a mischievous spirit getting in on the act. Remember you have free choice and you are supposed to live your life using your free choice. If you can remember what it felt like to be with the loved when they were living in the physical body you will still feel that same presence if they visit you either at home or through a medium. We all have a signature presence. That something that lets you know when someone you know and love is in the room. It is possible to feel the presence of not only someone who has passed over but also of someone who is on the earth plane even if they are at a great distance away physically. If you are close in spirit it is possible to travel to each other. Remember we are not bodies with spirits, we are spirits with bodies and time and distance are an illusion.

People who are recently bereaved often comment that they can still feel the person who has passed over around them. Our loved ones are often loath to go on until they think we can cope without them. They just want us to know they are okay and they still love us. We should let them move on and not bind them to the earth plane with our grieving. Prolonged grief is painful for us and painful for them to watch. If we allow grief to hold us in its grip, we do not fully participate in life on earth. I know it is easier to say than do, but, I believe it is good to grieve well and thoroughly and then continue with the business of living.

CHAPTER 4 CRYSTAL WORKING

Crystals and stones found their way into my life despite my resisting them. Whilst we were holidaying in Germany during July 2001. One morning at breakfast my husband showed me an article he read in a German newspaper promoting the use of crystal lamps and describing how people found them beneficial for their health, and how they could operate as a stress buster. The newspaper showed photographs of large lumps of quartz and fluorite with holes cut in them into which tea light candles were dropped so that when the candle was lit the light shone through the stone. The news article then went on to tell a little bit about crystal healing and the energy of stones. I read the article and thought to myself 'What a load of rubbish'. There was no way I was going to get into that crystal nonsense! The fact that my sceptical husband, he who shunned all things esoteric or holistic showed me the article should have told me that this was something I needed to take note of. I dismissed the article and enjoyed the rest of my holiday.

On the morning of 18th August that same year, during my morning meditation I found myself floating along flatlands looking at a village. I recognised the village and knew it to be in France (although I had never visited that country) I just *knew* this place. In the moment of recognition I was so shocked at finding myself there, I immediately came back to the here and now with a bang. An hour later I went into town to collect two books I had ordered from a local bookshop. Whilst waiting for my order to be found I idly browsed along the shelves, I took down a book on meditation as I returned it to the shelf a book on crystals fell off the shelf above and I caught it. I flipped through the pages admiring the photographs of various minerals and thought how pretty they were and vaguely wondered if there really was anything in all this 'crystal stuff' finally I decided to buy the book out of curiosity to see what it was all about. As I paid for the books I had ordered and this other one, I wondered what on earth I was doing parting with good money for a book on a subject, I had no interest in. As I stepped out of the bookshop I found myself looking directly at a stall selling crystals! I was certain it was not there when I entered the bookshop. However, as it was early in the morning and I had spent some time in the store, I presumed that the vendor had arrived whilst I was making my purchases. Out of curiosity I stepped forward to the crystal stall and thought what a strange coincidence it was that I should have just bought a book on the subject and here was somebody selling them, synchronicity again. I walked up to the table of fascinating, glittering and shiny stones and purchased a tiger's eye and a citrine. I noticed some clear stones marked as blue obsidian, I picked one up and remarked to the man selling them that they looked green to me. The woman working on the stall who I had, until then not noticed came up to me and said she agreed, they always appeared green to her too. She then proceeded to show me a book she owned and said she thought I should purchase a copy it was about crystal healing. She was rather insistent that I needed the book and wrote down the name of it, the author and ISBN number. Again she urged me to purchase a copy even though she did not sell books herself. I smiled and nodded whilst inside my head I was thinking to myself "you must be joking. I'm not having anything to do with this stuff". She then went on to tell me that one of the crystals I had purchased would help to ground me and she thought that recently, I had probably been off travelling in my dreams a lot, she said she thought this might have frightened me. As soon as she said this, I remembered the vision of the French village and told her of the experience. She smiled and looked at me with her clear blue/green eyes and I felt a connection with her. This was my first meeting with Crystal Anne our paths crossed many times afterwards. Anne informed me she thought I had recently experienced some eye troubles and the stone would help with that. I felt sure she was right, however it was not ordinary vision she was talking about. I used that stone many times during meditation and it was a wonderful tool. Eventually I sent it to a very dear friend, as I felt that this stone had finished its work with me.

Having purchased my first couple of crystals from Crystal Anne and her husband, and my first book on the subject from the bookstore, I soon found that crystals started to feature greatly in my life but purely on a personal level, they were not to become part of my healing work for some time. My bookshelf started to brim over with reading matter on how to work with them, and other surfaces in our house became littered with crystals and stones. With practice I learnt to meditate with stones to find out where they originated. Imagine the joy of asking a stone to show you its birthplace and being taken right into the heart of a volcano. I also discovered that through meditation and intent it is possible to meet the crystal's diva, sometimes they appear as one might imagine a fairy might look but even more beautiful, other divas take on very different forms. Once connection is made with the crystal if one asks, it will show what its purpose or life task is. Certain ones will wish be used as meditation tools, others healing aids and some for scrying. Most people tend to think of quartz spheres (otherwise known as crystal balls) as being scrying crystals but there are others which also make excellent 'seeing stones'. I have a two-inch polished quartz point with a cut and polished base which at one time I often used for this purpose, I used the face and sides of it.

It took a long time for me to remember the multi-faceted crystal given to me by my guide and to understand the significance of what he was giving me. Now I understand he wanted me to work with these wonderful earth gifts. As I have already said, at first I was only using crystals for my own personal use. Suddenly it seemed as if crystals were everywhere. I became aware of them in shops I had not noticed before and I received wonderful crystals as gifts from friends and family. I still have some of the crystals I purchased in the early days; others have left me after a very short period of time. It became clear to me that we are only their earth-keepers for the length of time they need to be with us. It can be very sad to part with a crystal one has a great fondness for. I once had a small piece of blue kyanite I used to hold it to balance my chakras and those of people who came for healing. I found that if I asked clients to hold it during the healing process, my job was made much easier. Blue Kyanite will balance the chakras automatically without one using intent and with intent can be used to open up the chakras. Kyanite is one of the two crystals I know of that never need cleansing I kept this piece of blue kyanite for several years it lived on a small round table in the study/healing room. I never carried it with me until one morning I felt compelled to pop it into my pocket shortly before leaving for work. That morning I had a meeting with Christine who was the first of the three who told me that I should become a healer, as we sat talking I kept sensing that I was being prompted to give her the piece of blue kyanite. As it was a stone I was particularly fond of, I tried to ignore the promptings. The harder I tried to dismiss the urge to give her the stone, the stronger I felt a whoosh of coldness down my right side this continued until I could ignore it no longer. In the end I gave in to the wish of spirit and begrudgingly handed it over and explained to her what an excellent balancer of energies it was. I was rewarded firstly by the coldness down my side dissipating and secondly by, her telling me she had recently experienced problems with balancing her chakras. This gave me the confirmation that it is always better to listen to spirit rater than one's own selfish desires. We cannot own crystals despite paying money to purchase them, but we can have the pleasure of their company and, if we are lucky, we can work with them. Not many weeks later I came across another piece of blue kyanite set as a pendant which felt right to me and I purchased it, in fact this one suited my purposes even better than the first as I was able to wear it on a chain thus having it with me at all times. I prefer to carry crystals I need with me in my bra, this places them next to my skin and in the area of my heart chakra Kyanite is not a smooth crystal and in my experience not at all comfortable to wear in ones bra so sometimes a piece of jewellery is better.

At the same time as I purchased the first piece of kyanite I bought another one, this piece was very pretty and contained a lot of mica which gave it a wonderful spangled effect, as soon as I took it home I popped it into a little wooden box where it remained for several years, occasionally I peeked at it but never used it as a working crystal, I knew it was not for me, sometimes it crossed my mind that I would never find the person it needed to go to but eventually I did. A teenage girl came for a healing session; the crystals in my room fascinated her. Shortly before she and her mother left after a treatment I showed her the pretty kyanite piece, her eyes lit up and I knew it had found who it wanted to go to, she bore it off home in its little box and I felt very happy to have had the opportunity of uniting the two. There is something very satisfying about helping a crystal find its next home even though it may not stay with that person for long.

Several of my stones came to me firstly in dreamtime. Each time this has happened I have met the stone within 48 hours of having dreamt of it. Once I dreamt about a beautiful string of quartz chips, my husband purchased it for me the following day at an alternative health fair, I still love that necklace. Although he came along to the fair begrudgingly and moaned and groaned all day apart from when he was making sarcastic comments, it was he who found the advertisement for the fair in the local newspaper in the first place. Considering he has always been very sceptical to say the least, several times he has been the catalyst for my taking steps in my journey. Whilst at that fair I met a very wise old lady who gave me some information I needed to hear and without which I might well have taken a wrong turning on this journey.

The strangest crystal I dreamt of was what appeared in my dream like a pale flint arrow head. The next day I walked into a crystal shop and there were two of them sitting on the shelf, pieces of calcite looking for all the world like arrow heads I purchased both of them and they still sit waiting for the time we are to work together although I suspect one of the two is for myself and the other for someone else.

Sometimes we just know we have a special crystal that will stay for a long time. I do not make a habit of giving crystals names, but, I do have a very special one known as Bernard. One day my friend Paul and I attended a psychic fair. On the publicity material it was stated that crystals would be available for sale Paul had seen the advertisement and asked if I would like to go, as he knew I had become interested in crystals. In fact there were very few crystals for sale. Only a couple of small baskets of polished, pebble sized crystals and one amethyst cluster measuring approximately three by four inches across. Its points were quite chunky and very, very dark and lacklustre it appeared to have an almost black coating on its points. I picked it up and remarked to Paul what a sad looking thing it was. Three times I went into the room where it was, picked it up and put it down again. Paul laughed at me each time, and made comments about how expensive it was, and how he hoped I was not going to part with money for such a sad looking lump of amethyst. Each time I assured him I was not. On my fourth visit to look at the sad amethyst cluster, I felt such a pull to it and a thought flashed through my mind. I asked the woman selling it, if she knew who had been using this cluster. She looked uncomfortable and glanced at her friend. They both stood and looked at me for a moment, and then one of them spoke to the other. "That's the crystal John borrowed" (The name may not have been John, but it was a man's name they used.) I asked if this person they were talking about worked on the Light or dark side. One of the women replied that when they first met the man who, had borrowed the crystal he seemed, really nice, she used the phrase 'Like Mary Poppins in trousers'. However, they had since discovered he was anything but the lovely person he was thought to be, however, they did not know what he had done with the crystal or what he had used it for only that he had borrowed it for a while. Listening to them it crossed my mind that to lend a crystal to a person was a very odd thing to do. Whilst we were talking a Reiki master came into the room and listened to the conversation. She invited me to accompany her into the next room with the crystal so that she could dowse it. The diagnosis was not good; although there appeared to be some energy it was badly depleted. She laid down the pendulum she was using to dowse and told me, it was a sick crystal, adding that she felt if anyone could improve its energies I could. So, very much to Paul's amusement I paid far too much money and took the poorly crystal home. There are tried and trusted methods of energising crystals, but I worked from my own intuition. It just happened that we were having some very high winds accompanied by heavy rain at the time. The first thing that I did when I arrived home was to place the crystal outside in the garden. There it stayed for 48 hours, with the weather driving and whipping out any negative energy. Over the next few weeks, the amethyst cluster was laid in sea salt water, sunshine and moonlight (amethyst should not be put into sunlight for too long as it fades), I took it to a holy well and dipped it in the water and then to my favourite little waterfall to wash out any remnants of negativity, and to wash in love and light. I felt that this crystal had come to work with me and I was determined that it would be restored. I took it with me to work daily and placed it on my desk. Over several months it was handled by many women all who appeared to fall in love with it on sight. Without being invited to hold it, they just instinctively picked it up from my desk, I noticed that once they held it they seemed to have great difficulty putting it down. The healing energy of the women who held it was, definitely an important part in the crystal's rehabilitation. It was one of these women who named it Bernard. I admit that although it has a gentle quality, Bernard does seem to have more masculine than female energy, so the name suits it. It was wonderful to watch this beautiful crystal transform from something that appeared dark and dead to alive and glittering. This crystal's work to date, has been mainly working with people who have emotional problems.

Bernard was in fact my second 'rescue' purchase. In September 2001, whilst visiting a seaside town in County Wexford on my first short trip to Ireland I purchased two small quartz points from a new age shop. Like Bernard, they looked so very sad and dull. I just had to liberate them; one had been made into a key ring with a metal pin securing it to the ring by the pin penetrating into the crystal, the other one was just very dull and unhappy looking. When I saw these two crystals I experienced the same feeling one might have on seeing a child mistreated. As soon as we were out of the shop I demanded that my husband remove the key ring pin. Although up to that point the only method of cleansing crystals I knew of was by holding them under running water and asking three times that all negative energy flow from them, turning them around and asking three times that Love and Light enter them, I instinctively knew that these two crystals needed to be put into seawater, when I told my husband that I wanted to put them into salt water I was both amazed and grateful that instead of scoffing at me he immediately suggested we go to a local shop and buy a bottled drink which we could empty out and fill with water from the sea. I purchased a bottle of juice, emptied the contents and went to the beach to fill the bottle up with seawater. The two crystals were then popped into the water and the top returned to the bottle. The crystals remained in the bottle of seawater for several days until I returned home. Like Bernard they were also treated by stays in sunshine and moonlight and carried around by me. I sometimes use these now happy crystals when I lay a Star of David formation around people who come for healing.

That first trip to Ireland in itself was strange. My husband had always wanted to visit the 'Emerald Isle' but I had always refused to go. It was not just a lack of interest in visiting Ireland, each time he mentioned it I felt a panic and dislike of the place well up inside of me. I was vehement in refusing to go. We had always promised ourselves a special one-week holiday for our silver wedding anniversary. We said we would visit somewhere warm, and a stay in a nice hotel. Throughout our married life due to the lack of money our holidays had been of the camping or caravanning variety plus visits to family in England when we lived in Germany, and visits to family in Germany when we lived in England. As the anniversary of our marriage drew nearer we started to discuss where we would go, we considered many destinations including Malta, Italy and Madeira. One night my husband told me I should decide where we were going before it became too late to book anything, I don't know what made me say it but the response that shot out of my mouth was. "Ireland, I want to go to Ireland and stay in bed and breakfast accommodation". I remember the look of amazement on his face as he reminded me that it was one of the places I did not want to visit. I merely said, "Well, I want to go now". So, Southern Ireland it was, and we both fell immediately in love with the place, the people, the landscape and the food.

We decided to spend the last couple of days of our holiday in the county of Wexford. Early one evening we went for a walk on a beach. I noticed a wooden bench on the entrance to the beach with writing on it. To my amazement I read 'Sli Charman'. Charman was my maiden name. Not trusting my own eyes, I asked my husband what it said. He confirmed that I had read it correctly, I then noticed a map of the area on a notice board, and there it was again. On enquiring at the local pub, I was told that Sli means path or way, and Charman was the old name for Wexford. Sli Charman is the Wexford coastal path. My husband laughed and said that my family must have originated in the area. My parents divorced when I was six years old, however, I had kept contact with my grandparents until they passed over both of them lived well into their nineties. There had never been any talk of Ireland. My grandfather came from an army family; he was born in Woolwich in London and had never really known his parents as they went wherever the army sent them, leaving my grandfather and his brothers to be raised in army boarding school. When we returned home we showed my sister the photographs of the bench and map, she was as surprised as I, and refused to believe it had anything to do with our family, but my husband gently pointed out that our grandfather was a dark haired blue eyed man, a look known to be common amongst the Irish. I am aware that there have been people by the name of Charman in England for several hundred years but, I will round this story of by telling you that approximately twelve months prior to my visit to Ireland, I had a reading done by an Irish woman who had told me that my family were from Ireland and had gone through very hard times. Now I regretted having laughed at that woman because at the time I thought she was talking a lot of nonsense. If you pay good money to someone for a reading, listen to what you are told and do not disregard anything you are told it might not make sense at the time but may do so at a later date.

Two years later my sister who lived in a town approximately 45 minutes' drive away from where I was living at the time, telephoned to inform me that, her local college was running an evening course on crystal work. At first I was interested in attending with her, but later changed my mind deciding it was too far to drive every week during the winter months and, I really did not want to have to face the resistance I was sure I would meet from my husband if I told him about the course. I did however mention it to him the only response I received was a non-committal sort of snort and tut. I also used my dowser to see if I needed to attend the course and got a resounding no. This did not surprise me as I had by this time read a great many books on the subject and, although I was not using crystals in my healing work I knew that I could if I chose to. Then one evening my husband and I were eating our evening meal when suddenly he asked me when the crystal course was going to start, I glanced at the calendar and replied that it was that night, he commented that if I was going I should get my skates on. I really did not have time to get there, but rang my sister to see if she was still going. I am sorry to say I embarrassed her by telephoning her during the first session of the course, however the tutor allowed her to answer her telephone to speak to me. I had thought the lessons would commence at 7pm when in fact the starting time was 6pm. Between them my sister and the tutor encouraged me to jump straight into my car and drive to the college which I did, leaving my dinner uneaten on the table.

On reflection the response from my dowser in saying I did not *need* to attend the course was correct; the fault lay in my asking the wrong question. I should have asked if I *should* attend the course. Apart from speeding up the acquisition of some knowledge and the fact that I passed the course and obtained a diploma in holistic crystal therapy there was definitely another reason that I was guided onto that course.

One of the students was a very outgoing and likeable woman who was a medium and very involved in the spiritualist church. She did not complete the course, in fact she did not attend many sessions, but, she was with us long enough to tell me the name and telephone number of a crystal wholesaler. This took my friend Paul who was at that time also a colleague, and myself, onto another adventure altogether. Paul was a real joy bringer and whenever we were together we tended to spend most of our time giggling and being rather silly. Paul and I had started to chat about crystals, he had some huge quartz points he had owned for some years and had done some crystal working, but his path was very different to mine as were his methods of working. One day I mentioned to him that I knew of a fairly local crystal wholesaler through my course colleague and we decided to pay a visit him together. We went several times and were delighted to discover that although the vendor did not normally sell to individuals he was happy to sell to us. After a few visits and many crystals added to both of our collections we chatted about how much fun it would be to have a crystal stall, after much discussion and investigation we discovered we were able to hire a trial stall within a shopping centre in the town near where we worked. The stall was a small barrow of the type often used by flower sellers. Unfortunately as a one off trial we were only able to hire the barrow for four consecutive days including a weekend, the shopping centre which owned the barrows were not willing to hire out on Saturdays only. We organised our time off between us, living in dread that our employer or his wife would see us. On reflection we had very little stock and not a great selection, but we did sell enough crystals to turn a small profit. Even more importantly to us, we had great fun talking to the public and other stallholders. This had given us a taste for the business, so we set about finding a more permanent pitch to sell our wares. It took us several weeks but eventually we found there was a vacancy for a Saturday market stall in the small town where my sister lives. The other stallholders must have thought we looked ridiculous on our first day at the market. Our 'pitch' was a trestle table on the outside part of the market. So we found ourselves at the crack of dawn on a wet and windy Saturday in January trying to make the trestle table look inviting. We had a nice black cloth to show up the quartz. As we set up stall that morning we tried to use drawing pins to hold down the cloth as the wind howled around us, in the end a lovely man who sold fishing tackle on the stall next to us came across and threw half a dozen clamps onto our table with a gruff "here you better use these" I think inwardly he was laughing his socks off at our attempts.

We spent the day in the freezing cold constantly re-lighting the incense sticks and the candle in a hurricane glass which we had taken along because we thought it would give 'atmosphere' to our stall, and having taken them there, we were adamant we were jolly well going to use them! I think that first Saturday was the worst weather we ever experienced on the market, it rained, snowed, hailed and the lazy wind (one that goes straight through you because it is too lazy to go around) was cruel. It was also one of the best days of my life! Customers came and purchased and even more importantly chatted to us despite the bitter cold winter weather. That day we made one wonderful conversion to the world of crystals. A young couple with a baby came up to the stall, the wife was interested in the crystals but the husband was very sceptical, I discovered he had a painful shoulder caused by his work as a scaffold erector. I passed him a small, flat citrine pebble, which is one of the crystals that does not require cleansing (blue kyanite being the other). I asked him to tape it to his shoulder using the type of surgical tape that looks like paper; I would take no payment from him but asked him to let me know how he got on with it. He agreed to try the crystal but made it clear to me he did not expect it to work. His wife assured us she would make sure he used it. The following week he was back telling us how amazed he was at how much the crystal had helped him. I remember laughing and informing him that I did not tell lies. He became our most frequent customer calling in to see us every week if only for a chat, he also built a wide collection of Jasper pebbles amongst other stones, which he purchased from us and other sources. He often popped in to show us a crystal he had found elsewhere, several customers had a habit of doing this, we were always interested in such purchases and pleased that customers felt comfortable enough with us to show what they had bought from other crystal sellers, although we did sometimes laugh together and comment on the likelihood of people taking a nice cabbage purchased at one greengrocers to another shop to show what they had and getting the same reaction as they did from us when we examined their purchases from other vendors. Occasionally customers brought us gifts, wonderful little treasures including crystals for one or the other of us, sea shells, and one person even gave us a lot of paper bags to pop our customer's purchases into thus saving us having to buy them. Now, where else could one work in retail and have customers present one with gifts? We also gave gifts. Now and again we met somebody who one or both of us felt needed a certain little crystal and it was always gifted.

We had a wonderful eighteen months on that market stall. After just a few weeks we were offered an indoor stall at a reduced rate, for use over the winter months. Once summer came around someone else wanted the stall for handicraft goods and as they were willing to be open all week and not just Saturdays we found ourselves, back outside again, but, this time under a tin roof for which, we were grateful on cold wet days. The outside part of the market had once been the local cattle market, this amused me as my family had originally come from the area, I was aware that, some of my ancestors would have taken their farm produce and beasts to that very market. I wondered what they would have thought about me selling stones where they sold their carrots and cows. The tin roof gave some shelter on wet days but also drew the heat on sunny ones. In the Autumn, we were offered another indoor stall, We had a ball of a time, ours was certainly the prettiest stall on the market, not just because of the crystals but because we kept decorating the stall. For example we had pumpkin lanterns at Halloween, stars and moons all over the place at Christmas, hens and chicks for Easter, not to mention the silver stars Paul stuck all over the lavender coloured material that lined the walls, we purchased a beautiful colourful sari which got used over and over again in different ways as decoration. The other stallholders would often wander down to see what we were up to. We used to watch them drift down casually glancing at the wares on the other stalls until they came to look (sometimes stare) at ours. We were aware of the smiles and merriment we caused. Our view was if we gave them something to smile at, we had brightened somebody's day, our job was done.

We made many friends on the market, some of the other stall holders were very kind to us, for example someone gave us a portable heater, and someone else gave us some fabric material for the stall. The customers to the market were wonderful too, many people called in just for a chat and bit of counselling, and we felt very honoured that strangers let us into the intimate parts of their lives. One lovely man used to pop in each week to tell me a joke, he never purchased anything but that was by the by, he brought me something to smile and laugh at, in return I listened to him talk about his younger days and his grown up daughter who had moved aware from the area with her husband and children. We became a place for folks to gather and chat I know that customers became friends with each other over a piece of hematite or moonstone.

One Saturday afternoon a middle-aged woman came to the stall and announced that she had come for two things a certain type of crystal and some healing, which she almost demanded from me but, in such a nice manner I was happy to be of service. As it happened Paul, was not able to work on the stall that day, so my sister was helping me. I agreed that after I had driven my sister home at the end of the day I would go to the woman's house. I am still taken aback when perfect strangers even 'sensitives' recognise me as a healer without being told that I am one. It was an interesting session and the woman and I became friends exchanging information with each other for a while until we finally faded away from each other.

Eventually we gave up the market stall because we wanted to undergo some training in hypnotherapy and the study days fell on weekends. We split the stock as neither of us had room to store it all. The market manager assured us we would be welcome to return in the future. We were certain that we would be back at some time. Unfortunately we never got the opportunity to resurrect the business for two very sad reasons. The market was closed down and the space it occupied sold for building purposes and secondly Paul died of cancer aged 45. I will be eternally grateful for the years I had the best colleague and friend a person could wish for. Paul I thank you for the fun and laughter.

Try it yourself
There are lots of great books on working with crystals, which crystals to use for various purposes, how to do a crystal layout etc and there is lots of information on the internet. I am going to make some suggestions how to choose a crystal and how to cleanse it. I always cleanse new crystals.

Choosing crystals;
If you see a large array of crystals but don't know which you should buy, simply go for the one that catches your attention so long as it is within your price range.

Some people find it helpful to stand in front of a collection of crystals, close their eyes and relax then open their eyes quickly and pick up the first crystal they see. Sometimes we see a crystal and just know it wants to be with us at least for a while. They do not always stay with us, sometimes we are just temporary Earth Keepers for a while, then we meet someone and instinctively know it is for them. If you are choosing a crystal for a specific purpose such as meditation or healing, just hold that intention in your mind and project it to the crystals you are looking at. Some people sense an energy from a crystal, this might be a flash, a vibration, resonance, a tingling , a euphoric awareness or a sense that the crystal is jumping up and down saying to you "take me, take me". If you are choosing a crystal for another person visualise that person and project that image onto the crystals and see which one jumps out at you. Sometimes we see a crystal and just know who it is for. We have all been seduced by a pretty or flashy looking piece like an ornate dowser or wand that we never ever find a use for.

Cleansing Crystals;
1. There many ways of cleansing crystals including;
2. Take the crystal to the sea and letting the water wash over it, then allow it to dry and energise in the sun.
3. Go to a waterfall or stream and again letting the water wash over it, then energise in the sun
4. Hold the crystal under a running tap or water poured from a container
When I use any of the above, if the crystal has a point I hold it point downwards if not just hold it and say three times "May any negative energy flow from you" I then turn it around so that the point turns upwards and say three times (water still flowing over) - "May Love and Light enter you".
5. Soak the crystal in sea salt for 7-24 hours then rinse in pure water. Salt may mar the surface of some crystals although it will not affect it's properties.
6. Using a glass container soak the crystal in saltwater for between 1 and 7 days. Make up a solution of of about three tablespoons of salt to one cup of water (approximately 235 ml or 8 fl oz). The solution should completely cover the crystal. Place the container with the crystal in the saltwater in a location that receives sunlight.
7. Placing the crystal in brown rice for 24 hours. The rice is said to balance and centre the energy removing any negativity. Some people are said to eat the rice afterwards believing that it is also purified and energised. Of course one would need to make sure

that no fragments of mineral such as mica was left in the rice.

8. Smudging by burning dried herbs and wafting the smoke over the crystal, smudge sticks can be purchased or homemade.

9. Laying the crystal on an amethyst bed. Amethyst is said to transmute lower energies into higher frequencies.

10. Burying the crystal in the earth, the earth is said to have a natural magnetic quality which draws negative energy out of the crystal. Take care to mark the spot where you bury the crystal or bury it in a pot full of earth or you will never see it again.

11. Use sound, a resonating bell, singing bowl, wind chime, Tibetan symbols or a tuning fork hold the crystal within the sound

12. A very fast and easy method is breath cleansing simply using your own breath. Firstly clear your mind as much as possible then holding the crystal in your fingers gently blow on it with the intent of removing and negativity. As the negative energy is removed imagine that negative energy being absorbed into the ground and being transmuted into positive energy for the greater good of all.

I like to energise my crystals by putting them out in the moonlight when we have a full moon. Some people like to put theirs out in sunshine near water.

CHAPTER 5 WORKING WITH OTHERS

The following poem is often circulating social media, I have tried but have been unsuccessful in finding out who wrote it. Whoever it was, I thank them. I ask you to read it now.

Reason, Season, or Lifetime

People come into your life for a reason, a season or a lifetime.
When you figure out which one it is,
you will know what to do for each person.
When someone is in your life for a REASON,
it is usually to meet a need you have expressed.
They have come to assist you through a difficulty;
to provide you with guidance and support;
to aid you physically, emotionally or spiritually.
They may seem like a godsend, and they are.
They are there for the reason you need them to be.
Then, without any wrongdoing on your part or at an inconvenient time,
this person will say or do something to bring the relationship to an end.
Sometimes they die. Sometimes they walk away.
Sometimes they act up and force you to take a stand.
What we must realise is that our need has been met, our desire fulfilled;
their work is done.
The prayer you sent up has been answered and now it is time to move on.
Some people come into your life for a SEASON,

because your turn has come to share, grow or learn.
They bring you an experience of peace or make you laugh.
They may teach you something you have never done.
They usually give you an unbelievable amount of joy.
Believe it. It is real. But only for a season.
LIFETIME relationships teach you lifetime lessons;
things you must build upon in order to have a solid emotional foundation.
Your job is to accept the lesson, love the person,
and put what you have learned to use in all other relationships and areas of your life.
It is said that love is blind but friendship is clairvoyant.
— Unknown

I truly believe that when people work together in pairs or groups they can move mountains There have been several interesting studies done on the power of prayer in aiding healing such information is readily available via the internet for instance in 1988 physician Randolph Byrd released his findings from a study carried out five years earlier on the power of prayer on cardiac patients. In his study 85 percent of patients who were prayed for by the allocated prayer groups scored good on the hospital's rating system used to rate response to treatment compared to 73.1 percent of the 'non-prayed for patients. This study launched a spate of similar studies some with similar findings, some with the opposite. There is a problem with this sort of study because it cannot be completely controlled. There is no knowing if the patients in both the prayed for and non-prayed for group are being prayed for by friends and family outside of the study. Some of them may have friends who are Reiki Masters or using similar other healing modalities who would send them healing. There is also the matter of the patients soul contract. It might be their time to exit this lifetime. However, I and other I know have noticed that when a group of healers work together the energies certainly appear to be very powerful.

There have been several studies on the impact of large groups of transcendental meditation (™) practitioners carrying out mass meditation. One such demonstration of the power of ™ was a carefully controlled scientific experiment carried out in Washington between 7th June and 30th July 1993. The maximum reversal in predicted violent crime trend was 23.3 percent which was at the point when the most ™ practitioners were involved. Of course the crime rates returned once the meditation experiment stopped

I have found that my relationships with other spiritually minded folk are different to relationships I have with other people. There can be a depth of understanding which is hard to describe whilst, at the same time one does not get caught up in pettiness, jealousies or romance. I think this is because the relationship is based on spiritual awareness and usually a desire to grow and learn. I have often found that the people I have spiritual based relationships with are people I believe I have met in past lives. You just know at first meeting that you are of the same 'tribe'.
Working with people you have never met in this lifetime might sound strange but if we remember that everything is energy and energy can move faster than light, distance is of no importance.
The Internet has been a wonderful tool to bring like-minded people together. I have been lucky to meet and work with many wonderful people via this medium. I think I should add one word of caution here. People are not always who they say they are. People can invent any persona they want to on the internet, they can pretend to be someone other than who they say they are. It is very easy to invent an avatar which is why we hear stories of children and vulnerable adults being groomed and conned and in some cases this has lead to actual abuse. On the other hand we can also become paranoid and ultra-distrusting of others. Use your instincts but also check people out if you can. The use of Skype and other such face to face communication tools has made it harder for some individuals to hide their true identity.

I have had some fascinating experiences working with people in other countries including the use of telepathy, not only to send and receive mental images but also smells and sounds. One friend in Texas was given a box of oranges, for days I could not understand why I was smelling oranges when we had non in our house, when I mentioned it to her she told me about her box of that fruit and the amazing scent they were giving her house. On another occasion I kept getting the scent of almonds and coffee, always around lunchtime on work days. It turned out to be the time another friend caught up with their email whilst enjoying an almond pastry in a coffee shop.

Sometimes things went awry, for instance one friend and I were indulging in what we called remote viewing but, was probably more like telepathy. Like the woman I mentioned earlier this friend lived in Texas. We agreed a day and time to work together, on this occasion I was the receiver. Imagine my surprise when all I 'saw' was a straw duck. I reported back what I had 'seen' and was very disappointed to discover that the image that had been sent to me was a Cardinal, which I believe is a pretty red bird common in North America. We don't get Cardinals flying around Worcestershire so I guess a straw duck was what my comprehension had made of it. Our brains try to make sense of what it receives from our senses. On reflection I may not have been so far away from the truth. In fact I have never seen a cardinal so would not have recognised it, what I got was a different sort of bird, I also think spirit was laughing and having a joke with us. At least they did not show me a table, wristwatch or even a high ranking catholic official. The lesson in this for me was not to think I am so very clever and to work within known boundaries.

One friend and I worked together as healers even though we lived nearly 5,000 miles apart. In addition to sending each other distance healing which we did from time to time, my friend and I often shared names from our healing list so that people got a 'double' dose. When my sister had to undergo a surgical procedure, I asked my friend to send her some distance healing, and somehow they picked up on the thing she needed most, which was calming energy. I received an email the day prior to the visit to the hospital to tell me my sister would be sent calming energy. I drove to my sister's house that evening having offered to stay with her for a couple of days, which meant I could take her to and from the hospital and look after her following the procedure. On my arrival she confessed to me how anxious she had been feeling about the procedure and what else the doctors might find, and how during that afternoon all of the anxiousness had suddenly melted away, I just knew that my friends calming energy had worked. As I had not informed my sister about my friend's intentions to send energy and she had no other way of knowing about it, this was certainly not a case of 'mind over matter'. My sister not only sailed through the procedure but the doctors found absolutely nothing wrong with her, even the fibroids which they had seen at an earlier appointment had disappeared!

Because of the time difference in our two countries it was hard for my friend and myself to be awake and working on spiritual matters at the same time. For a long time we spoke about doing a synchronised healing session. Finally one Saturday morning at 06.30am my time 12.30pm Texas time we worked together on a handful of the people on my list and one from theirs. Not only were the results for the clients very good, there was also an effect on our healing rooms. We both found a change of energy in the part of the room where we had done the work from. After our session I found that when I did healing work in the area the air felt charged with energy and made my fingers tingle even more than they normally did during a healing session my friend reported a similar change in their healing room.

Sadly that friend passed away in the summer of 2014, but I have no doubt the work continues on the other side.

Anne the crystal seller who I mentioned in the previous chapter of this book was also involved in a new complimentary medicine centre that was opening in a nearby town. She invited me to the grand opening when members of the public were invited to wander around and learn about the services on offer. She and I were sat discussing the various therapies, life in general and our recent spiritual experiences. I told her that I was still aware of visiting France during meditation sessions. She asked me if I had ever heard of the Cathars, I had not, but as soon as she said the word, a huge wave of sadness gripped me I felt myself shaking and had to hold back tears. This emotional reaction to a strange word made absolutely no sense to me at all. Naturally I asked Anne what a Cathar was but she just asked me to look up the Cathar castles on the Internet. Imagine my surprise when on doing an Internet search I saw the photograph of the very same castle built high on a cliff that I had seen many times in meditation. There were two castles that looked very familiar. Without saying why I wrote to my friend in Texas I had shared the healing session with and asked them to look at the site. The reply I received was that there were two castles that were very familiar and they had something to do with one of our past lives. My friend had of course picked out the same two castles as I had. Reading about the slaughter of the Cathars explained my reaction to hearing the word. It also went some way to explaining one of my phobias…fire. I have had a fear of fire all of my life. The Roman Catholic churches way of getting rid of the Cathar people was often by mass burning them in huge pyres. Information regarding the beliefs of the Cathars is thought to come mainly from those who were tortured by agents of the church of Rome and therefore probably not very dependable however we do know that they were Gnostics and believed in a simple secular life and opposed the hierarchy imposed by the catholic church. Six months after learning something of the history of the Cathar people, I attended a mind, body and spirit fair. I was talking to a man who produced elixirs for many types of illness. He was talking to me about how people bring physical complaints and phobias from past lives into their present life. He looked at me and said, "For instance if you had been burnt, you may come into this life with a fear of fire". I admitted that I had a fear of fire, he nodded and told me I had been burnt to death on at least two occasions in France. There is maybe an extra twist to this tale as there often is. My mother and I carried out a study on our family tree. We discovered that in the seventeenth century an ancestor by the name of Elizabeth Munford married into our family. Munford is a derivative of the name DeMontford. Simon DeMontford was a Frenchman who won the battle of Evesham (1265), a town not far from where Elizabeth Munford lived and married. Simon DeMontford was the son of a French knight of the same name and the man who was leader of the crusade against the Cathars organised by Pope Innocent III. Elizabeth may have been a descendent of that family, or her ancestors may have been amongst DeMontford's men. I wonder if there is some karmic influence at work within this?

Sometimes spirit work with us as individuals but we get affirmation of the message by talking to someone on the earth plane. One evening in meditation a man came to me, he told me he was known as Jeff, but his name was really Ben. He said he was going to take me on a journey of a lifetime. He certainly did that, it is very hard to describe where he took me, but there were huge billowing, tumbling, colourful clouds and lots of activity caused by silent explosions causing silver dust to float around. The best I can describe it as is, it was like being inside a gigantic pot of magical soup. I asked Jeff where we were he laughed and told me I was being shown worlds being created. He spoke to me about many things, which I am sorry to say I could not remember afterwards, at the end of the journey he said again his name was Jeff but really Ben, and told me to ask one of my American friends about him.

The following evening I went to my beginners' course on astrology, which I was attending at a local college. It was a cloudy night so we were not able to go outside for any stargazing; I was very disappointed about this until, the lecturer produced some fantastic slides of nebula where stars are born. Basically nebulas are immense clouds of gas and dust in interstellar space. I was looking at slides of exactly what Jeff had shown me I had never heard the term 'nebula' prior to that evening but I knew exactly what I was looking at.

Two days later I had the opportunity to mention Jeff to the person he had told me to speak to. They affirmed yes, they had a cousin by the name of Ben who hated the name and was known as Jeff. Sadly Jeff had passed over at an early age. I have never seen Jeff since but I have never forgotten the amazing journey he took me on out to the nebula. I am certain if I had not been carrying out distance work with his cousin, Jeff would not have taken me on that journey so it is important that we work with other people because the connections and experiences can be greater than we expect them to be. Besides working with others means we have company on our journey which is far more fun than traveling alone.

CHAPTER 6 DREAMS & ASTRAL TRAVEL

Dreams
I think people have been fascinated by dreams ever since time began. We know that the Egyptians, the Ancient Greeks and other early cultures set high store by the importance of dreams, and of course dreams feature in the bible. I am certainly not an expert on dreaming and as, there are many books on the market that explain the reasons we dream and even more that offer analysis and interpretations of the symbolism of dreams, it is my intention to merely share with you a couple of my dreams that have been important in my development. I am certainly not going to vie with great minds like Sigmund Freud, Carl Young, Alfred Adler and Erich Fromm all of whom had strong views as to why we dream and the functions of dreams. I will say though that in my experience some dreams make sense of what is occurring in our life and help us to sift and sort events, highlighting those things, which we may wish to pay attention to, including our hopes, aspirations and fears helping us integrate information and our emotional states. And I believe that some people have prophetic dreams.

On my bookshelf there are a couple of books to be found on the meaning of the symbolism of dreams, I do from time to time refer to these books however, I have learnt, that generally it is for me to understand my own dreams although outside help can be helpful. I have found that if I use reference books to discover the meaning of certain symbols in dreams, I have to also take into consideration what is happening in my life at that time, and the emotions

I experience within the dream as well as the events that occur in the dream. I have from time to time tried to keep a dream diary but must confess I am not as good as I should be about keeping it up-to-date. Sometimes my dreams are not for me at all but for another person the following is an example of this.

I started to dream of a child, at the outset he was the most beautiful baby; I dreamt I was playing with and cuddling him and thoroughly enjoying being with him, I knew he was not mine but loved him nonetheless. I had read that to dream of a child is to dream of our own inner child so for example if one dreams of a neglected child it might be because we are neglecting our own inner needs. As the nights went on the child started to grow, he grew from a beautiful baby into being a delightful toddler, we continued to enjoy our time together, however, as the dreams continued and he got older I became more certain this was not an inner child dream and other symbolism came in and I got the feeling the child needed some sort of help. Then came the night when the child was looking for his father, in the dream I promised to help him with his search, during this dream I remembered to ask the child his name, and he gave me a clear reply. I spoke to someone I knew who did work on soul rescuing which is taking spirit who are trapped in this dimension home. He was certain the child needed to be taken into the Light and he told me that the next time I saw the child I was to tell him it was time to go home.

At the time I was dreaming of this child I belonged to a spiritual group on the internet who discussed dreams. Something inside my head told me there was a connection between this child and that group. I decided to ask if any of the group were dreaming about a child and it appeared that several were, my next step was to ask them to find the name of their child, replies came flooding back but nobody had the same child as I did.

The next stage in this story was the most amazing for me. One morning I did a meditation during which I saw a woman give birth to a very beautiful child, I then watched the child die and be taken away, it was the most heart breaking of scenes and upset me greatly. I wrote to the group and told them about it, I also told them the name of the child in my dream. It was a rather unusual name. Can you imagine when I received an email back from one of the members telling me that the child was her son who had died 40 years less one week from the day of my meditation? She told me she had spent the past 40 years grieving for that baby who only lived a matter of hours after birth. As group members use pseudonyms there was no way of linking this child to the woman. Besides, in her email she mentioned she had remarried following a divorce and the surname of the child would not have been the one she currently used. She also told me that her first husband who was the child's father had passed over following their divorce, which may have explained why the child was seeking him. The most humbling part of all this for me was the woman thanking me for having looked after and cuddled him in my dreams and for seeing him safely home.

The learning in all of this was to be willing to share information with other people, had I not shared this with the women in the group that woman would never have known her child was now safe. However, I do wish I had shared the information earlier, as I am sure that given the opportunity she would have wanted me to pass a message to him, of course he knew she loved him.

Another dream, which involved a child, helped myself and another woman become close friends. We both belonged to the same, social network group as with other groups that I have belonged to it was a closed group which means that only invited people are allowed to join and, in common with other social network groups I have belonged to, the majority of the members are either Native Americans, part Native Americans or have an interest in Native American teachings.

In my dream I was scared of something although I did not know what, I was in a room and had a key to the door, I saw the lock very clearly there was a pin in the centre of the lock and I had to put the key in so that it fitted over the pin, I managed to carry out the task just in time. Then a small dark haired swarthy looking man appeared over the top of the door it was as if there were walls and the door but no ceiling. I told the man to go away but he said that James had sent him to help me. I did not believe him, and then he gave me some numbers that I knew were associated with my birthday but was not quite my date of birth. This was one of those dreams that play on one's mind and I just could not shake it off. I was chatting to a friend on the Internet and mentioned the dream to him remarking at the same time that I did not know anyone by the name of James. The friend reminded me that we did have a James in our social network group the husband of one of the female members, the wife was a frequent writer to our message board but James seldom did because he was often away from home due to his career, in fact at the time of my dream he was away from home for several weeks and his wife and I had been writing to each other frequently during this period of time. My friend thought that I should contact James' wife and tell her about the dream so I did wondering if she would consider me completely potty for having done so. She replied that the dream made her think of doors being bolted whilst horses had flown and that this was much as she had been feeling for the past few weeks. At the end of her email she wrote: 'Um...... something just hit me........What IS your birth date? I'll tell you why if it clicks ok?' Naturally I replied telling her my birthday what I wrote was 'My date of birth is 04.07.1951 I soon received my friend's reply part of which was as follows:

'I thought that might be why I was curious, but you MUST keep this secret PLEASE as even my James does not know yet. I am pregnant and due (I Swear this is true) on April 7 of next year'. When I read this it took me a while to work out the significance, once I had, I wrote back: 'Wow I just went very cold as I read this the second time, why the second time? The first time I read it I was confused why you were talking about April 7th. Over there (USA) 04.07 means 7th April yes? Over here it means 4th July! Now here is an odd bit, when I wrote to you at first I typed 4th July then changed it to 04.07.1951 and wondered why I was doing so, obviously you needed it in the way you would understand.'

The rest of this story and what happened during this pregnancy is not my story, sufficient to say my friend and I communicated and worked together intensely for a while. The relationship was mutually beneficial during our email discussions I told my friend about a dream when I was asked to choose a stone and had the message "Elizabeth this is your people you are Hopi" my friend wrote back and told me that I had been in the women's Kiva. My friend taught me that a Kiva is the name the Hopi give to their ceremonial rooms which are basically a room which is wholly or partly subterranean and entered via a ladder. Apparently women go into the Kiva to choose a stone that will inform them of the path they are to take. They do this twice firstly when they reach womanhood and again when they reach the age when their families have grown. My friend recounted that she had once worked for a man who was Hopi and he had told her much about the Hopi way. More recently I have read of how the Hopi people were given stone tablets with hieroglyphs cut into them very similar to those carved in Egyptian temples. Having looked at drawings of these tablets through search on the Internet they are familiar although I could not say they are what I saw in that dream. Sufficient to say I have since then become very interested in the Hopi and the Hopi prophecies.

We returned to Ireland for a week to celebrate my 50th birthday. I had an interesting experience during a meditation session on the morning of my birthday, a man appeared to me, he talked of music and encouraged me to sing. I am absolutely tone deaf, people only ask me to sing once, and they usually soon ask me to stop! I do however love listening to music. He also told me that he was going to help me. That night we went to a local pub that was advertising live folk music. The notice outside of the pub door proclaimed the music would start at 7.00 pm. We sat and drank our Guinness and, from about 8 pm the musicians slowly drifted in one by one carrying their instruments and gathering at a table, they chatted and drank and actually started to play at about 8.30 with more musicians drifting into the pub and joining in as the

night wore on. One of these music makers was a tall, young, long-haired man, who reminded me greatly of the man in my vision. Actually, he looked exactly like him. It was a wonderful evening and because the pub was so packed out and the music so loud I felt free to join in with the singing safe in the knowledge that none could hear my off-key voice. Near the end of the night, the tall longhaired young man came over to chat to us I noted we were the only people he made a point of talking to. He was no Irishman. This chap was Dutch. I was delighted to speak to him as I have had a love affair with Holland since I first visited the country in the early seventies. Over the years we have spent many holidays in Holland. When he took his leave of us I said goodbye, he shook his head and insisted I say the Dutch parting words, which mean 'Until we meet again'. I have not to date met him since, but would not be surprised to see him pop up at some point. The additional twist in this tale is, I belonged to an email group of like-minded people interested in spiritual matters. We took turns dreaming for each other, I had requested that the group dream for me for my birthday. When I returned to England from the Irish trip I was surprised to find that several of the group had caught a dream for me, each of them reporting dreams of people offering to help me just as the man in my vision had! Synchronicity again?
I
certainly believe that we do sometimes travel during our sleeping time. For several weeks in 2001 I went through a period of feeling very tired when I awoke, I knew I had been dreaming about hospitals but could not remember what I was doing. One morning I awoke from what I believed to be a dream, the only part of the dream I was able to recall was looking down at my night dress and feeling embarrassed to be out and about in such shabby night attire but then thinking, "It's okay they will not mind at all". I had no idea who I meant by 'they'. A couple of days later I had a reading from a woman who was a stranger to me, she asked me if I was aware that I was doing what she called 'rescue work' at night. On questioning she explained that I was helping people who had passed over in the night to their next stage. The information this

woman gave me certainly explained the vague recollections of hospitals I had and if she was correct, I am sure the souls I was working with were not going to be too worried about what my nightdress looked like. However, you can be assured that it made me reassess me sleepwear. I certainly wished I could remember more of where I had been and whom I was with during those hours but I can only presume that there was no need for me to remember the details. I don't think I have been involved in rescue work for a while. Remember the spiritual work we do today can be very different from what we do tomorrow. We must be willing to be flexible, if we are progressing we are given different tasks so nothing stays the same.

Have a go
Try keeping a dream diary. It can be great fun keeping a dream diary, sometimes we get insight into our lives by looking back at our dreams over a period of time. Keep a notepad/book close to your bed. It might seem a good idea to keep your notes on a computer but if you wake up in the middle of the night by the time you have opened up your pc or laptop you will have forgotten half of the dream. Some people like to use a voice recording gadget but if you are going to do an analysis of your dreams over a period of time, you do need to have the information written in one format or another. Some people find it helpful to use an unlined writing pad or notebook if they want to add sketches to their notes.

Before you go to sleep set your intentions to remember your dream.

As soon as you wake up make notes including; everything you experienced within the dream especially including how you felt during the dream. Don't worry if you only remember fragments of your dream. What you remember will be what you need and all will become clear. The more you practice the better you will be at recording your dreams.

Astral Travel

There is much talk about astral travel occurring during dreamtime. I have often woken feeling very tired as if I have been busy all night. At other times I have had dreams that feel so real that I have wondered if I have actually been out and about astral travelling. This occurs especially after those dreams when one can still remember the feel of things and people encountered and touched in the dream. I certainly know that when I slam back into my body I have certainly been out of my physical body and have been brought back in a hurry. Probably because of a noise in the bedroom such as my husband turning over in his sleep has jerked me back. I really do not like that thudding back I always feel as if I am going to go right through the mattress.

It would appear that aspects of us can also move around in the daytime not just at night, on many occasions I was seen by people at work who were certain they saw me in one location when in fact I was in a very different place. For example, two people simultaneously watched me walk from the training room across a well-lit hallway and into my office. When in fact I never moved from the training room where I was participating in a meeting. On another occasion I was talking to someone on the telephone who suddenly became silent and then demanded to know "How did you do that"? Apparently I appeared stood right next to her for a fleeting second. She was located approximately 15 miles away from me at the time. My friend Paul did not actually see me but he was certain, that I entered his house one evening. The following day he told me that he had sensed my presence and could even smell my favourite perfume which in those days I wore all the time. During 2004 there seemed to be a lot of this 'flitting about' not only did numerous people claim to have seen me in locations other than where I was, I heard several reports of other people experiencing the same phenomena and I also had experience of it myself as a recipient. On two occasions I heard my husband arrive home from work an hour before he actually reached our house. I heard the key in the door, I heard the door open and close and I heard him call "Cooee" as he always did on returning home. On a further occasion from the kitchen window which looked out to the road approaching our house I saw and heard him ride his motorbike down the road and stop outside the house half an hour prior to him actually arriving. We lived in the end house at the bottom of a cul-de-sac so I could not have mistaken another motorbike rider to be my husband because there was nowhere to go past our house and the motorbike did not go back up the road besides I knew my husband's bike because it was a very large vintage BMW tourer. On all three occasions I was not expect him home until later so it was not a matter of seeing and hearing what I was anticipating.

Another occasion when I was told I had astral traveled was in November 2004. My daughter and I went to Egypt on holiday, we spent a week in Cairo. Like many people I had always wanted to see the pyramids and the sphinx at Giza. It was a very special holiday. Apart from the sites we saw, I had my daughter to myself for a whole week also it was the first holiday when I stayed in a hotel. The luxury of not cooking, cleaning or doing any laundry for a whole week was wonderful. During 29 years of marriage we had lovely holidays in both the UK and mainland Europe but had always stayed with family or in caravans, chalets or our battered old Volkswagen camper van. It was also the first time I had been on an aeroplane after 30 years.

We arrived in Cairo late at night, both feeling very excited at the prospect of our adventure. We were taken to our delightful hotel and were thrilled at the luxurious room with its elegant ensuite bathroom; once we had settled in we decided to have an early night in readiness to rise early the following morning for our first sightseeing trip. As I settled down into bed I was suddenly gripped with absolute terror as realisation set in that here we were, two women, a very long way from home, in a very foreign country where we did not speak the language or understand the culture. I remember thinking to myself "I can't just get home" I was scared and for once in my life did not know what to do. I had put myself into a situation over which I felt I had no control. I was then struck by the thought that I could go home in spirit. I closed my eyes and imagined the view of the back garden from my bedroom window. I immediately fell asleep waking up the following morning to the sound of the alarm clock. I felt as if I had only just closed my eyeshot sleep and could not believe the night had passed so quickly and was amazed at how deeply I must have slept. I remembered nothing of my dreams. The feeling of homesickness from the previous night had faded away and was forgotten for the rest the holiday.

On our return to the UK, my husband collected us, from Heathrow Airport. We dropped my daughter off in Portsmouth at the ferry port so that she could return to her home on the Isle of Wight, and we proceeded back to the Midlands. As we made our journey home I chatted to my husband about the holiday and the sights we had seen. Suddenly I remembered those few awful moments of fear and homesickness on the first night but omitted to mention how I had fallen asleep thinking of the view of our back garden. I only told him I had been terribly homesick on the first night. My husband glanced at me and said very quietly "I think you came to see me". With a little prompting from me he described how on that first night, he had been awoken by the sensation of someone floating down and laying besides him and a hand that reached out and touched his arm. Apparently he had been surprised but not at all scared. Once he had recounted to me what he had experienced I understood why the fear of being so far from home had melted away and why I had remembered nothing of my dreams that night. I am certain that I did in fact astral travel home that night and having done so my higher self was able to tell my sub consciousness that there was no need to feel separated from home. I felt that this was a massive breakthrough for my husband who was always such a sceptic but the greatest surprise to me was how calmly he had accepted the event. I was also very surprised he told me about what he had experienced. However, when I tried to return to the subject with him several days later he denied any knowledge of what I was talking about.

My astral traveling did once earn me a scolding from my mother. On one of the occasions when my dear step dad was admitted to hospital, prior to my going to sleep I set my intention to send healing during my dream time. The following day my sister and husband took the early visiting slot. On their return to my home they informed me that our step dad had told them that I had been floating around him during the night. Apparently my sister had replied that I probably was and that was the end of the conversation. That evening I drove my mother to visit the hospital. During the drive home my mother suddenly asked me if I had been floating around Worcester Royal Hospital the previous night. I said I might have been which earned me a strong reprimand from my mom and instructions to 'Never do that again!' He had told my mother about my visitation while I was purchasing something for him in the hospital shop. He had mentioned it to mom in a matter of fact way, not at all worried apparently he found it very comforting that I was there, but my mom's fear was that if he told the nurses his daughter had been floating around him all night they might think he was elderly and confused, hallucinating and change his medication. Sadly my mother was correct, in our culture we do not accept that spirit can be seen and those who do see or hear spirit tend to be labeled either as crazy or delusional. I often think of a story a friend of mine told me about when working in mental health. He heard of a woman who kept remarking all morning about the men in the trees outside her room. The care staff humoured her a little then became exasperated as she continued talking about 'the men in the trees'. She was told that there was no-one in the trees and given a little extra medication to help calm her because the more she was told there was no-one to see in the trees the more insistent and agitated she became. Eventually one member of staff glanced out of the window and surprise, surprise there were two tree surgeons at work in the trees outside the woman's bedroom window. Just because we don't see something doesn't mean it isn't there.

From the types of experiences of astral travel I have outlined above, questions arise such as how can we be in two places at once? Well, we are told that everything is an illusion. Part of the illusion that we all conspire with is that we are bodies with souls. This is untrue, we are souls who have chosen to surround ourselves with bodies of density that matches the density of the other things we have built into our sophisticated illusion such as houses, furniture, cars, etc.

Everything is connected and part of the same field. I find a good way of understanding this is to think of an ocean, a huge body of water, but that body of water is made up of tiny droplets of water. Each droplet is part of that huge body of water individual and at the same time part of the whole and connected via the vibration of the tides. Some people use the analogy of the cells of the body each cell is as important as all the others, each cell has it's own function as do we, all the cells are tiny but they make up the whole and all are connected by the same life-force.

CHAPTER 7 PSYCHIC ABILITIES

I will mention seeing events before they appear to happen, however, I certainly do not consider myself to be very gifted as a clairvoyant. Clairvoyance is the gift of clear sight. I am convinced that there are those people who can truly see events before they happen. In some cases it can of course, be beneficial for individuals to be warned of what might be popping up in their lives in order for them to either prepare for such events or to take damage limitation action. However, maybe we should not spend too much time looking into the future because in doing so we are not living in the here and now. I truly believe in the old adage that yesterday is history tomorrow is a mystery this moment in time is a gift which is why it is called *the present.* Our time on this plane is short and we should make the most of and savour every second. If we knew exactly when our marriage is going to end or a dear member of our family is going to pass over, would we really take time to smell the roses or watch a spectacular sunset or would we only focus on that fateful date in the future?

Throughout history we have had seers who have been shown the future, as I have already stated I do not consider myself to be a clairvoyant however, along with the other gifts I have been blessed with I do have warnings when something (usually unpleasant) is going to happen but I am not tuned in very well into understanding such warnings. Rather than being clairvoyant I tend to be clairsentient which means clear sensing. Such warnings can be a duel edged sword. I will give you a few of the most extreme examples I have experienced.

During the summer when I was 11 years old I had an uneasy feeling all summer long that something was going to change and my life was going to be different but I just could not put my finger on what was going on. At the time I was living in the Shropshire countryside with my mother, my younger sister, my mother's sister who was only five years older than me, my mother's mother and my grandmother's brother. It was a happy household and I loved my home and family. There certainly was a big change about to happen at the end of the summer months. My mother remarried, which meant that my sister and I were uprooted and taken to live in a town in Worcestershire. I had to leave my beloved countryside and even worse my darling grandmother who I called Nanny, I was devastated. Although throughout the summer I had sensed changes were coming I did not know what they were and still enjoyed the summer. Had I known what was going to occur I suspect I would have spent the summer in floods of tears making myself and everyone else unhappy instead of which I was running wild in the meadows and enjoying the freedom of the countryside.

In August 1999 my husband, daughter, nephew and I spent our summer holiday in Cornwall in the South West of England. A couple of days before we returned I had a strange tingling sensation in the area of my solar plexus, it was most unpleasant and even woke me up at night, I had no idea what was causing the discomfort. At the end of the holiday we drove back to the Midlands arriving home very late at night. The following morning when I awoke and went downstairs, my husband was already up and watching the television in the lounge. I stumbled bleary eyed into the room, as I greeted my husband my attention was caught by the scenes on the TV. The picture was of Buckingham Palace and a flag at half mast, sombre music was being played. I asked my husband if the Queen Mother had died and was stunned at his reply "No Princess Di" Somewhere deep inside of me I knew that the feeling I had been experiencing in my solar plexus was connected to the death of Princess Diana. Sure enough I did not get that feeling again until 2001. All through August and into September that year the horrible tingling which was at times downright painful in my solar plexus kept making itself known to me, waking me up at night. It was not there all the time but was intermittent throughout the days and nights. The difference this time was instead of feeling it inside of me it was about a foot away from my actual body, but, I could still physically feel it. I know this might be hard to understand if you have never experienced it yourself. What I was feeling was the solar plexus working overtime in my auric field. On the morning of September 11th I woke up and realised it had stopped, it felt as if it had gone for good, not a trace left. I breathed a sigh of relief and relaxed until the news of the twin towers and the horrific scenes we are now all familiar of hit our TV screens.

That horrible painful tingling was with me again on 23rd December 2004 this time accompanied by lots of ringing in my ears, it continued until Boxing day 26th December when again the world was devastated by dreadful news, this time the Asian Tsunami. Those huge waves that ripped in and took so many lives.

So, the question is why do we get these warnings? What are we supposed to do? Could we stop these catastrophes? I believe the answer to this question is no. It is not up to us to stop these events, it would be impossible, we cannot and if we could, we should not interfere with the Universal Plan. No more than we can stop the road accidents which we may see happening in dreamtime or in mediation. What we can do, is pray for, or send healing energies to those concerned. If all Light Workers do their little bit we can alleviate the suffering of those involved and their families.

I started this chapter by talking about seeing events before they *appear* to occur. Let us not forget that some people believe that there is no past present and future but everything is occurring at once.

I am not an adept clairvoyant, when I am shown things I have difficulty in interpreting what I am seeing. Some years ago I kept getting an image of someone I knew at work, each time I saw her, she was lying on the ground with what appeared to be a head injury. I remember talking to a friend about this, I was worried that the woman I was seeing on the ground might have a riding accident as she was a keen horsewoman but I knew that I could not ask her to stop riding. In fact, I had not interpreted what I was seeing very well at all. Not long after I had started to see this image of her on the ground she was dismissed from her job and had a nervous breakdown. So, what I had seen was prophetic however not at all what I had interpreted the picture I was shown, to be. I cannot help but wonder if I had meditated and asked my guides for help would I have had a clearer picture and could I have done something to stop the final outcome. I will never know.

It is not only the sitter, but also the person who goes for a sitting, that can misunderstand what is being shown. I remember once giving a reading for a friend. It was one of the first readings I ever gave, I was clearly shown a packed suitcase at the bottom of some stairs. The person I was doing the reading for informed me that her parents were going on holiday so we agreed that this was what it was about, I kept being shown this suitcase and then was shown coats thrown down on the bottom of the stairs, so I asked if anyone had a habit of doing this, she replied yes her brother so I asked her to tell him this was not a good thing to do as someone might trip on the coat and take a tumble. What I missed at the time was the fact that I was only shown one suitcase; both of her parents were going on holiday. Not long afterwards her brother left his wife. I did not listen attentively enough to spirit, if I had done so I might have been given further information. If I had listened better and if we had understood the message we could not have changed the outcome, but, the person I did the reading for, may have been better prepared. She was very upset by the breakdown of her brother's marriage which affected the whole family. This was a lesson in cockiness for me.

Of course it is not all doom and gloom, sometimes, we are given nice things to see, for instance a young woman I knew was pregnant and having a very difficult pregnancy, which looked like it was heading towards a miscarriage. I was shown a beautiful little girl playing on a swing. I was lucky enough to speak to the pregnant woman on many occasions throughout the pregnancy and did my best to encourage her to look forward to bringing a healthy baby into the world. She did indeed give birth to a beautiful little girl a healthy child who now attends school.

As I stated at the start of this chapter, I am not good at clairvoyance and have no wish to be because life is supposed to be an adventure, I also believe in self fulfilling prophecies for example a young woman who is told she will marry a tall dark haired man might turn down dates with blonde man of medium height because she knows he isn't 'the one' and by doing so miss out on a wonderful experience. I don't want people to tell me the plot of a book before I read it and being told what is going to happen in my life is similar however, I do understand that sometimes we need reassurance that things are going to work out okay or to get some sort of guidance.

I am certainly not saying you should not develop skills in this field if you wish to do so. I would urge you to find a good teacher. You can also do exercises on your own. One of my favourites games as a teenager (and occasionally now) was when walking in an urban area to guess the colour of the next car to come from behind where you are walking.

I strongly believe that everyone has psychic abilities it is just that some people have developed theirs more than others, this might be through natural development, or development through study and practice either is equally valid. I find it easier to think of so called psychic gifts as 'senses' or abilities because the term gift insinuates that only certain people have these abilities gifted to them.

Some people have a natural propensity to use one or two abilities whilst others use more. Some people find that when they open up to using one of these senses/abilities they develop other ones. Everyone can develop and use these senses/abilities if they choose, on the other hand we can also choose to turn them on and off. The following are my short explanation of the common terms used regarding what are termed 'psychic abilities'.

Clairvoyance - This means clear-seeing, in my experience the clairvoyant may work in a variety of ways, they might see people who are in spirit, angels, entities and auras. They may see visions which means seeing images either moving or still. Their eyes might be open or closed the images can appear to be seen with physical eyes but are most often to be seen on the 'screen' inside the head as with a dream. Other terms used to describe a person who is clairvoyant include seer or a person with second sight another term that is often loosely used is that of psychic. I believe that clairvoyance is becoming more common, the first encounters of seeing spirit is people seeing just a flicker of something out of the corner of the eye or thinking we have seen someone fleetingly but when you look again there is nobody there. People who see images of events before they happen are using clairvoyance, people who see images of spirit are using clairvoyance.

Clairsentience - this means clear-sensing/feeling. If you have ever had a gut feeling about something and been correct in that feeling, you have experienced clairsentience. We talk about gut feelings. The person who has developed this sense is very sensitive to the emotions of other people and energies which is why they are often referred to as sensitives or empathic or empath for short. A person who is empathic can also pick up other people's aches and pains. If this happens we should acknowledge the fact and ask for the discomfort to be taken away from us and for the person to whom it belongs to be helped though whatever is happening with them.

Clairaudience - this means clear-hearing. The person who uses this sense may hear all sorts of sounds that are not of the physical plane including voices of people who have passed in spirit, spirit guides, angels, whistles and buzzing noises not caused by tints, music and sounds of past activity in buildings that they visit. I have noticed that a lot of people seem to report their first contact with spirit is hearing their name called when there is nobody else in the vicinity. I remember in 1998 I went through a period of hearing my name called. It happened once at night and several times on Sunday afternoons when I was about to take a nap. The voice sounded like my mother's voice but it had a strange extra clarity to it. I mentioned to my sister that I kept hearing what sounded like our mother calling me and to my surprise my sister replied that the same thing had occurred with her. One of the reasons we found this phenomena very strange was because our mother was still on the earth plane. My sister spoke about these events to a very wise old woman who asked if our mother was also in the habit of taking a Sunday afternoon nap, when my sister concurred that she was. The wise old woman's explanation made perfect sense to us. She suggested that our mother was astral travelling, probably completely unaware that she was doing so and her spirit was calling her daughters.

Claircognizance - this means 'clear-knowing'. The person who uses this skill will have knowledge of certain people, situations, and places; they often don't know how they know, they just do. It is not that they sense something they KNOW. A friend of mine told me that she suddenly found that she could look at somebody and know everything there was to know about them. This ability did no last long and as she told me she found it very uncomfortable I suspect she shut it down herself.

Clairalience - this means clear-smelling. In other words the person smells something that is not physically near them. It is not unusual for a person to smell the favourite perfume of someone who has passed over or the scent of their favourite flowers. You may have someone in spirit who smoked a pipe or cigars and you might smell the pipe tobacco or cigars when they are close to you. It is also possible to smell aromas from people and places that are not connected to you when spirits are about. It is just one of the ways that spirit use to let us know that they are close, in the same way as they might blow on you, touch you so you feel a hand on yours, they may even give you a gentle poke or, you may feel a tickling energy or cobwebs on your face. I have had my hair pulled on more than one occasion.

I would not want anyone to believe that being a 'sensitive' is all joy and fun. I would not like to lose the gifts given to me, but I do think it is only fair and in the interests of a balanced view, to point out some of the negative aspects of these particular gifts. Since my childhood I have been able to see and sense events prior to them occurring. I will give you a few examples. In meditation I have seen road accidents and fires before they have been reported in the press. One could say there are accidents and fires somewhere every day, but when I have seen road traffic accidents I have been shown the exact cars in the exact colours colliding in exactly the same order as shown on television. When I have seen a building on fire, it has not just been a fire, but the exact building that has burnt. A couple of years ago driving through France, I glanced skywards, my eye was caught by an aeroplane flying overhead, the thought went through my head that it could just drop out of the sky. A few hours later I was sitting in a motorway service centre. The restaurant was built so that customers were able to sit right over the motorway looking down at the traffic speeding by. My husband and I had a table that was by a window. This meant we had an excellent view of the traffic flowing in each direction. We sat eating and chatting, I glanced down at the traffic and in my mind's eye saw a car drive off the carriageway onto the central reservation. Sure enough seconds later a car did just that. Thank goodness the driver got out unscathed which is more than I can say for the poor sapling he drove into. The following day on arriving back in England I read that an aeroplane had fallen out of the sky somewhere over France. I have often heard people ask why individuals are shown tragedies before they happen. This question is most often asked by people who themselves have the gift of 'seeing' as it is very frustrating to see something awful happen before it occurs and feel powerless to do anything about it. If you 'see' a road traffic accident but you do not know the people involved or even the location of the accident what can one do? Besides even if you did know who the people were, they would probably not listen if someone tried to warn them not to take that trip. I firmly believe that if we do see events happening before they unfold there is a purpose. The purpose being we are able to influence the event insomuch we can ask that protective white light be put around those people who will be involved and we can call on angels/guides to be with those people at the time of the tragedy, and ask that anyone who leaves the earth plane during the disaster be taken home. Nowadays I rarely see such events prior to them happening but I am aware that the gifts we are given often change and sometimes they come in and out when least expected. Instead of seeing events before they occur, what I often experience nowadays is a very uncomfortable sensation in my heart or solar plexus chakra.

CHAPTER 8 FINAL BIT

The past few years I have been on a steep learning curve, I have learnt that if spirit wants us to work with them they will find a way of seeing to it that we do. I have also learnt that there is nothing to fear apart from fear itself. If we put ourselves into the hands of the creator then there is not anything to fear, and, the most important thing is to be true to ourselves. For when we are true to ourselves we free ourselves to do the work the creator/universe wants us to do. The biggest enemy is often ourselves and our own ego. We must never forget that our gifts are given to us and can be taken away from us. If we are lucky enough to be allowed to serve as healers, mediums, clairvoyants etc then we have a duty only to work for the highest good and we should never ever use our gifts as 'party tricks' no matter how tempting it can be at times for that truly is working from our own ego. Any spiritual gift given should at all times be only used for the highest good. I feel it is also very important for people to understand the limitations of the gifts given to them at any given time and equally important that they ensure that those they work with also know the limitations of such gifts. This will make dealing with people much easier. It is surprising how friends family and others can become very suspicious of the clairvoyant, medium or healer, suspecting that the person is going to read their mind or influence them in some way or another to their detriment or on the other hand expect them to know everything or able to remove all pain or suffering, and that is not possible. It is surprising how the old images of witchcraft are still within the psyche of many people with all the connotations that has. Worse still, we are sometimes expected, to work miracles which are out of the scope of the work we are supposed to do. This sometimes leads to people damn for example a healer as a fraud. Prior to agreeing to work as a healer either distance healing or 'hands on' I always inform the person making the request that healing goes where it is required which means the condition for example a back problem may be healed or the person who requires the healing may be given the strength to cope with the pain of the back condition. Sometimes it is the case that healing means healing into death. In other words, the person to whom the healing is channelled might pass over into spirit. Healing into death may mean that the passing will not be as scary or traumatic as it might have been without the healing. Some people may see this as an excuse, they might believe this is proof that healing does not work. Nothing will convince me, that healing does not work if, the person to whom it is channelled is willing to accept it at whatever level it is required.

Mediums can also be scorned by people who do not have their desires met. For example some people think that a medium can connect with *everyone* who has passed over, and that this can be done at the clients bidding, as if the medium has their own personal telephone line through to the spirit world. One can have empathy with someone who is bereaved and desperate to have contact with his or her loved one who has passed over. However, it may not be possible for the medium to make connection with a spirit and this can be for lots of reasons, maybe the person who has passed over does not want to have a connection with the person left on the earth plane any more than some people on the earth plane have no desire to have connection with those who have passed over. It may be that having spent time together on the earth plain, their tasks are completed and no purpose can be met by further communication. However, it is far more likely, that the person who is in spirit, is busy completing tasks on the other side or, are on the next part of their journey and are unable to communicate via the medium. It should be understood that we are busy with our lives on the earth plane and cannot always be at the beck and call of our friends and family and the same applies to those in spirit. They are not just hovering around during the rest of our stay here on earth waiting for us to put a call through via a medium. In truth those who are in spirit are often willing to speak to us but we must have respect for them and their new 'life'. Don't we expect respect from others for all we must do in our busy lives? Is it not sometimes difficult for us to find time to make a telephone call or visit? Aren't we sometimes out when

people telephone us? So if you are practising your mediumship skills, please remember to explain to the person who has come for the sitting that they might not get a message from the person they are hoping to hear from. In fact it often happens that a message comes through from someone we least expect to hear from.
When unforeseen events happen to people who are clairvoyant there is always some person who will quip "Well, he/she did not see that coming" followed by derisive laughter as if the clairvoyant should be able to see everything that is going to happen minute by minute. Even clairvoyants have to live in the 'here and now' and tune into their clairvoyance skills when they are working although it is a fact that sometimes they tune in automatically. And, in the same way that healing goes where it is required, the clairvoyant will be shown what they or somebody else needs to know to help them make the best choices in their actions. If we knew every step of the journey in advance, there would be little sense in us being allowed to come for this great adventure which we call life with all the experiences it brings.
Anyone deciding to open up to using spiritual gifts has to be prepared for the fact that not everyone else around them will necessarily understand or agree with their path or beliefs. They may even have to part company with people they are fond of, this might be their own or, the other person's decision. It can, at times, be a very lonely and rocky road we walk however, other likeminded people are sure to appear in your life, it is amazing how once we open up to spirit we can suddenly find ourselves tripping over other people who are on the same journey. Sometimes people we have known for a long time but who have never shared information about their spiritual beliefs surprise us by turning out to be companions on the same path. Each individual has free choice and must weigh up the difficulties that may occur against the amazing rewards that those who walk the path of Light
I have also learnt that help is always on hand if we only ask for it, we should talk to the creator/universe/angels/spirit which we can do through prayer and, we can listen to the creator which we can do through mediation. I believe that Angels are always wait-

ing to help us but, we must ask first and we should also take care with what we ask for. Sometimes we put out a request to the Universe then we immediately negate the request by little add-ons for instance "I would like a different job .... But I know I will not get one because...." or "I would like to be able to do such and such a thing but I do not think it possible because...." Or we think we are unworthy of what we are requesting. If we put out a request and it is what we truly want and that request is for our or someone else's higher good the request is granted. We should also be specific about our requests often when we put out a vague request it is often granted but maybe not in the way that we would wish or the ramifications are not what we have thought about. For instance you might think something like "I wish I did not have to drive this battered old car" then we get cross when the battered old car will not start in the morning. What we should have put out is a request for the help to find the funding for a better car. So when putting out requests be clear about what you are asking for, be specific, make the request, and then leave it alone until the wish is granted.

Sometimes we can be surprised at how quickly a wish is granted for instance, I greatly admired some little angel cards and asked to be helped to find some, one week later I was given a set as a gift . Not long later I was telling my friend Paul about another pack of Angel cards I had seen and said how much I would like a pack, two days later someone turned up with exactly that pack for me, she was turning out some drawers and found them. Apparently she could not remember ever having bought them! A third set was given to me shortly afterwards in much the same way. Of course I now have a duty to use these Angel Cards not only for myself but also when working with other people. It is often the little bits of what one might call 'magic' that give the greatest joy.

I believe that it is important that we give thanks for the good things in our life, the people we meet, the beautiful sunset, or a flower that lifts our spirits and gifts we are given, I can now say I am a healer and I am thankful and humbled to have that privilege, I am a crystal worker and I am thrilled to be able to work with such wonderful tools, I am a medium and I am grateful to be so honoured. Every morning before I get out of bed I give thanks for at least six things for which I have gratitude. I find this small practice greatly enhances my life by putting me into a mindset of gratitude.

During the past few years I have been very privileged, I have worked with some wonderful people both those on the earth plane and those in spirit and have had some amazing tools in the crystals that have come my way. I have had the opportunity to serve others in my healing work and have been very humbled by the success of healing sessions. I think one the most amazing of all was the healing work I was allowed to do in 2002 on a lady by the name of Linda in the USA. In the June I received an email from a delightful young friend by the name of Adrienne. Adrienne wrote and asked if I could send some healing energy to a friend of her mother's by the name of Linda it transpired that Linda was very ill in hospital and about to undergo major surgery. Naturally I agreed and called on my healing guide to help me. Several distance-healing sessions later I was urged to send Linda some crystals one of which was a small quartz cluster which I was very fond of. The crystals were dispatched to Adrienne with a plea that she should get them to Linda, being the sweet soul that she is, she duly took them to Linda's husband with a request that when he next visit his wife in hospital he should take them with him. Adrienne wrote back that Linda's husband had been impressed with the energy he felt from the crystals and although he thought Linda did not hold much store by such things he thought she would like them because they were so attractive, apparently Linda did indeed like them and was touched that someone so far away would take an interest in her. I continued to channel healing energy to Linda and she made progress. At the end of July I went to Germany on holiday for a couple of weeks, whilst away I did very little healing as I felt I needed to rest. Imagine my distress when on my return I found an email from Adrienne sent the day before telling me that Linda was very ill, it sounded as if the medical staff had very little hope that she would pull through also Eric had told Adrienne that the crystals I had sent had disappeared from beside Linda's bed. I went straight to work and asked my healing guide to go and work with Linda. I am very happy to be able to say that Linda pulled through and the crystals re-appeared beside her bed. The wonderful little twist to this story is that when she was recovered and family and friends talked to Linda about what had happened during the days when she was close to death she told them she had dreamt of an Indian Chief who had talked to her and how she had heard music. This of course had echos of what happened to me when I had my breast lump. Of all the Christmas cards I have received amongst the ones I treasured the most were the ones from Linda for, she was indeed witness to the miracle that can take place when we on the earth plane and spirit work together. Linda did make her way home a few years later but I believe she had several happy and fulfilled years. I hope she found the opportunity to be at peace before she passed over. Once we start to view our existence as the magical opportunity it is, whole new worlds appear. The most important thing is to be open minded (but remember the pinch of salt). I have found that the most important things for me are to strive to be in the moment as much as possible, to meditate regularly and most important of all to stay in the flow. What I mean by being in the flow is to appreciate everything in our life and not to struggle against life. The more we try to swim against the tide the harder life becomes. I am not saying don't work hard for what you want, I am saying don't put energy in feeling angry, bitter and unhappy because what you get back is more of what causes those emotions. If we concentrate on the good in our lives the happier we become and we receive more happy experiences. As I have already mentioned I go through my gratitude list every morning. As a Reiki Master I also remind myself of the reiki precepts which were the basis of the teachings of Mikao Usui who gave us Reiki over 100 years ago. Mikao Usui did not devise the precepts they have been used by Buddhists for centuries and give us way of bringing positive change into our lives. The precepts are as follows:

Just for today;
I will not anger
I will not worry
I will be grateful
I will work with diligence
I will be kind to others

'Just for today' brings us into the present moment. When we are in the present moment it is much easier to live by the precepts. Also it is no use us telling ourselves that we will never become angry or worry ever again that is too huge but we can work on 'just for today'. We would be foolish to think we will never experience worry or anger ever again, however, remembering this precept helps us to keep things in perspective and focus our energy on more happy, loving thoughts.

Just for today I will feel gratitude helps us focus on the positive things in our lives, the more we focus on positive things the happier we become.

Just for today I will work with diligence helps us to focus on our work, if we use this precept in conjunction with the others we appreciate our tasks more and appreciate what we achieve and other people respect us and our place in the world.

Just for today I will be kind to others helps us to see the goodness in other people which in turn is reflected back to us.

I truly believe that living by these precepts makes life much richer and magical. Try it for yourself and see what happens.

I hope you have found this book informative and the exercises useful if not as you read them, you may find that you return to them at a later date.

I hope you continue to develop your awareness and find it as rewarding as I have found my journey to be despite my reluctance. Yes it can be hard work, yes some people might think you crazy but it is what we are here to do.

Love, Light & Rainbows
Elizbeth R

ABOUT THE AUTHOR

Elizabeth R

Elizabeth lives on the beautiful Isle of Wight where she practices as a clinical hypnotherapist, advanced practitioner in EFT, Holistic Crystal Therapist and Reiki Master.

In this book you are invited to riffle through a collection of spiritual events that have occurred in the authors life and see if you can find the odd gem or treasure that will be helpful to you in your own psychic development some bits might just amuse you or you may take comfort in knowing weird stuff happens and you are not alone in your experiences. Amongst this collection of psychic bric-a-brac there are true stories of meeting with spirit guides, astral journeying, healing, working with crystals and messages from spirit. Elizabeth is candid about how she was reluctant to become involved with anything esoteric and how spirit never gave up until they persuaded her to embrace her psychic gifts. Today she is glad she did finally surrender and become a healer.
Most of the chapters in this book include some simple exercises to help you develop your own abilities.

Elizabeth R is a Reiki Master, Holistic Crystal Therapist, Advanced Practitioner of Emotional Freedom Techniques and a Clinical Hypnotherapist

Printed in Great Britain
by Amazon